Riches for the Mind and Spirit

RICHES FOR THE MIND AND SPIRIT

JOHN MARKS TEMPLETON'S TREASURY OF WORDS TO HELP, INSPIRE & LIVE BY

Edited by
JOHN MARKS TEMPLETON
with JAMES ELLISON

A Giniger Book

HarperSanFrancisco
A Division of HarperCollins*Publishers*

FIRST EDITION

Library of Congress Cataloging-in-Publication Data

Riches for the mind and spirit: John Marks Templeton's treasury of words to help, inspire & live by /
    edited by John Marks Templeton with James Ellison.
        p.   cm.
    "A Giniger book."
    ISBN 0–06–250865–2 :
    1. Life—Quotations, maxims, etc.   2. Religion—Quotations, maxims, etc.   3. Conduct of life—Quotations, maxims, etc.
    I. Templeton, John   II. Ellison, James
    PN6084.L53H65   1990
    082—dc20   89–46449
                                                                    CIP

90 91 92 93 94 MART 10 9 8 7 6 5 4 3 2 1

This edition is printed on acid-free paper that meets the American National Standards Institute Z39.48 Standard.

*To the unsung heroes
of the military and intelligence services
who gladly gave their lives for us
that our lives may be useful and free.*

CONTENTS

INTRODUCTION

At the age of four or five, before I started school, I learned from my mother that one of the greatest blessings given to humanity is the gift of reading. Much of the world's wisdom resides in the written word. From the Bible, from philosophers and poets, and from other writers, we begin to form a clear understanding of the spiritual and ethical laws of life.

The world's literature teaches us valuable lessons that no amount of money can buy. Those lessons are there for everyone. They are free and they are priceless.

My purpose in assembling this collection of my favorite choices from the great works of inspiration is to pass on to others my love of reading and my joy in learning the valuable lessons of life. Because this anthology is the result of my reading over a lifetime, it would be impossible to include all of the Bible passages, works of theology and science, poems, songs, hymns, sermons, learned monographs, speeches, and works of fiction and history that have helped shape my life and make it richer. I would need many volumes! I am moved to mention, however, that Ruth Stafford Peale and Norman Vincent Peale have inspired and uplifted me and millions of others through their magazines *Guideposts* and *Plus*. And, although I have been a lifelong member of the Presbyterian church, my mother imbued in me something of the spiritual philosophy of the Unity School of Christianity. I have benefited by reading the Unity books and magazines for more than sixty years.

But, you might wonder, what profit is there in studying the wisdom passed down to us? Why not simply live from day to day, taking things as they come? The answer is that our stay on this planet earth is a brief one and the time we are given to educate ourselves is all too short. For each person to grow spiritually, it is important to learn from others who may be wiser than we. From them, we can come to realize the impact of even a small gesture, word, or action upon another person.

One thing we learn from these wise people is that giving is a test of maturity. Those who are truly grown-up, give. The immature do not. It is wise to practice giving in every area of life. Give your feelings to others. Give money where it is needed and can truly help someone. Give attention. Give thoughtful, well-reasoned advice. If you are lonely, it's especially helpful to give. Give by taking on charity jobs or helping with fundraising. But—most of all—give thanks to the Lord for your many blessings. As Rabindranath Tagore put it so eloquently: "I slept and dreamed that life was happiness / I awoke and saw that life was service / I served and found that in service happiness was found."

To pursue that thought further, the wisdom we can find in these pages teaches us that happiness does not come *to* us, but *through* us. It is a journey and not a stopping place. Achieving a goal brings less happiness than working with inspiration toward a goal. Happiness comes through the work we do, the skills we struggle so hard to develop, the love and attention we show to others.

We learn, too, that happiness comes directly through prayer. The term "prayer" can mean *to trap a thought*. As one holds a thought in mind, it becomes a "state of mind," or a general attitude. It is important to remember that we're not products of circumstances or accident. We're the end result of what we think. Our thoughts influence our words, our deeds, what other people think of us, and whether or not they want to associate with us. If we hope to lead a happy and useful life, mind power becomes essential. We can then make our mind a garden of indescribably beautiful flowers instead of a weed patch.

Giving, happiness, prayer, and mind power are four building blocks in the formation of a fulfilled existence on earth. I hope that this anthology can help you live in a manner that perhaps has never been better expressed than in the Apostle Paul's Letter to the Romans (12:9–18, RSV): "Let love be genuine; hate what is evil, hold fast to what is good; love one another with brotherly affection; outdo one another in showing honor. Never flag in zeal, be aglow with the Spirit, serve the Lord. Rejoice in your hope, be patient in tribulation, be constant in prayer. Contribute to the needs of the saints, practice hospitality. Bless those who persecute you; bless and do not curse them. Rejoice with those who rejoice, weep with those who weep. Live in harmony with one another; do not be haughty, but associate with the lowly; never be conceited. Repay no one evil for evil, but take thought for what is noble in the sight of all. If possible, so far as it depends upon you, live peaceably with all."

Now that I have reached the point of putting together my own personal collection of inspirational passages, I've found the hymnal a worthy model to follow in helping me organize my material. In the topical index at the back of the book, entries are placed in one or more of the following twenty categories: *charity, courage, creativity, enthusiasm, faith, forgiveness, giving, happiness, hope, humility, love, mind power, perseverance, positive thinking, prayer, pride, progress, thanksgiving, willpower,* and *work.*

I've been a devoted user of the church hymnal since my early youth. For me it has been a powerful teaching aid as well as a source of pleasure and solace. Hymnals of all churches are filled with inspirational literature, but no one hymn has been more inspirational for me than "Take Time to Be Holy," which you will find in part two of this treasury, "The Power of Spirit." I have selected other all-time favorites, among them "O God, Our Help in Ages Past," I Am God's Melody of Life," and "All Things Bright and Beautiful." All religions have tended to picture God in limited human concepts, but some sense of His true infinity is expressed in the hymns included here. Although the words to these hymns are memorable, I feel that seeing them in context with their music lends them even greater meaning.

Many passages selected for this book have numerous applications and thus belong in more than one section. For example, I have included a moving chapter from Dr. Robert Schuller's book, *You Can Become the Person You Want to Be.* It tells the story of how a woman overcame grave physical problems—problems that could have left her bedridden and helpless—to the point where today, against all odds, she is a practicing psychologist. The reader who uses the topical index will find this passage under *courage*, *faith*, *hope*, *perseverance*, *positive thinking*, and *willpower*.

The words that provide us with hope, inspiration, courage, happiness, and consolation come from all faiths and represent writers from many places and from various periods of our common history. In many different ways these writers say that life is a magic gift and that God is always ready to radiate His love and wisdom through our thoughts, words, and lives. It is my hope that readers, especially those who teach young people, will draw inspiration from these words and that, in the areas where individuals may feel most in need of help, some passage in this collection will point the way toward a brighter and more useful future.

John Marks Templeton

TALKING WITH GOD

I

WHEN I was a small boy growing up in Winchester, Tennessee, Sunday school was an important part of my life. It was there that I began to sense the magical power of spiritual conversation. I learned that when God talks to us, His means of communication is the Bible. The great lessons of Jesus are narrated for our edification and, from Genesis to Revelation, light is shed on the mysteries of spritural existence.

It was in Sunday school that I was introduced to the Golden Rule. People of all faiths have been inspired and uplifted by its message, which is repeated in the scriptures of the nine major religions. It was in Sunday school also that I first read the Sermon on the Mount, which is at the very heart of the Christian gospel and should be studied and memorized by every Sunday school student. Both the Golden Rule and the Sermon on the Mount are included in this section. As an adult, I taught Sunday school in the Presbyterian church in Englewood, New Jersey. I helped all of my students memorize Luke 6:27–38, where God speaks to us of the most profound matters.

When we talk to God we reach Him through prayer. We tell Him of our hopes and fears; we express our desire to help others and to become better human beings. In the Bible passages and prayers that follow, we can explore and experience the vital dialogue that takes place constantly between God and humans.

Because I find that some Bible translations express their ancient meanings in words I like better than others, I have drawn on three versions: the *King James Version* (KJV), the *Revised Standard Version* (RSV), and the *New English Bible* (NEB).

GOD SPEAKS TO US

In the beginning was the Word, and the Word was with God, and the Word was God. He was in the beginning with God; all things were made through him and without him was not anything made that was made. In him was life, and the life was the light of men. The light shines in the darkness, and the darkness has not overcome it.

John 1:1–5, RSV

"But I say to you that hear, Love your enemies, do good to those who hate you, bless those who curse you, pray for those who abuse you. To him who strikes you on the cheek, offer the other also; and from him who takes away your cloak do not withhold your coat as well. Give to every one who begs from you; and of him who takes away your goods do not ask them again. And as you wish that men would do to you, do so to them.

"If you love those who love you, what credit is that to you? For even sinners love those who love them. And if you do good to those who do that to you, what credit is that to you? For even sinners do the same. And if you lend to those from whom you hope to receive, what credit is that to you? Even sinners lend to sinners, to receive as much again. But love your enemies, and do good, and lend, expecting nothing in return and your reward will be great, and you will be sons of the Most High; for he is kind to the ungrateful and the selfish. Be merciful, even as your Father is merciful.

"Judge not, and you will not be judged; condemn not, and you will not be condemned; forgive, and you will be forgiven; give, and it will be given to you; good measure, pressed down, shaken together, running over, will be put into your lap. For the measure you give will be the measure you get back."

Luke 6:27–38, RSV

But the fruit of the Spirit is love, joy, peace, patience, kindness, goodness, faithfulness, gentleness, self-control; against such there is no law.

Galatians 5:22–23, RSV

"My heart exults in the Lord;
   my strength is exalted in the Lord.
My mouth derides my enemies,
   because I rejoice in thy salvation.
There is none holy like the Lord,
   there is none besides thee;
   there is no rock like our God.

Talk no more so very proudly,
    let not arrogance come from your mouth;
for the Lord is a God of knowledge,
    and by him actions are weighed.
The bows of the mighty are broken,
    but the feeble gird on strength.
Those who were full have hired
    themselves out for bread,
but those who were hungry have
    ceased to hunger.
The barren has borne seven,
    but she who has many children is forlorn.
The Lord kills and brings to life;
    he brings down to Sheol and raises up.
The Lord makes poor and makes rich;
    he brings low, he also exalts.
He raises up the poor from the dust;
    he lifts the needy from the ash heap,
to make them sit with princes and
    inherit a seat of honor.
For the pillars of the earth are the Lord's,
    and on them he has set the world.
He will guard the feet of his faithful ones;
    but the wicked shall be cut off in darkness;
    for not by might shall a man prevail.
The adversaries of the Lord shall be broken to pieces;
    against them he will thunder in heaven.
The Lord will judge the ends of the earth;
    he will give strength to his king,
    and exalt the power of his anointed."

1 Samuel 2:1–10, RSV

The Lord is my shepherd; I shall not want.

He maketh me to lie down in green pastures: he leadeth me beside the still waters.

He restoreth my soul: he leadeth me in the path of righteousness for his name's sake.

Yea, though I walk through the valley of the shadow of death, I will fear no evil: for thou art with me; the rod and thy staff they comfort me.

Thou preparest a table before me in the presence of mine enemies: thou anointest my head with oil; my cup runneth over.

Surely goodness and mercy shall follow me all the days of my life: and I will dwell in the house of the Lord for ever.

Psalm 23, KJV

I will lift up mine eyes unto the hills; from
    whence cometh my help?
My help cometh even from the Lord: who hath
    made heaven and earth.
He will not suffer thy foot to be moved: and he
    that keepeth thee will not sleep.
The Lord himself is thy keeper: the Lord is thy
    defence upon thy right hand.
So the sun shall not burn thee by day: neither
    the moon by night.

The Lord shall preserve thee from all evil: yea, it
    is even he that shall keep thy soul.
The Lord shall preserve thy going out, and thy
    coming in: from this time forth for evermore.

Psalm 121, KJV

Have you not known? Have you not heard?
    Has it not been told you from the beginning?
    Have you not understood from the foundations
    of the earth?
It is he who sits above the circle of the earth,
    and its inhabitants are like grasshoppers;
who stretches out the heavens like a curtain,
    and spreads them like a tent to dwell in;
who brings princes to nought,
    and makes the rulers of the earth as nothing.
Scarcely are they planted, scarcely sown,
    scarcely has their stem taken root in the earth,
when he blows upon them, and they wither,
    and the tempest carries them off like stubble.
To whom then will you compare me,
    that I should be like him? says the Holy One.
Lift up your eyes on high and see
    who created these?

He who brings out their host by number,
    calling them all by name;
by the greatness of his might,
    and because he is strong in power
    not one is missing.

Isaiah 40:21–26, RSV

Let not your hearts be troubled; believe in God, believe also in me. In my Father's house are many rooms; if it were not so, would I have told you that I go to prepare a place for you? And when I go and prepare a place for you, I will come again and will take you to myself, that where I am you may be also.

John 14:1–7, RSV

When the poor and needy seek water,
    and there is none,
    and their tongue is parched with thirst,
I the Lord will answer them,
    I the God of Israel will not forsake them.
I will open rivers on the bare heights,
    and fountains in the midst of the valleys;
I will make the wilderness a pool of water,
    and the dry land springs of water.
I will put in the wilderness the cedar,
    the acacia, the myrtle, and the olive;

I will set in the desert the cypress,
>   the plane and the pine together;
that men may see and know,
>   may consider and understand together
that the hand of the Lord has done this,
>   the Holy One of Israel has created it.

Isaiah 41:17–20, RSV

Who is a God like thee, pardoning iniquity
>   and passing over transgression
>   for the remnant of his inheritance?
He does not retain his anger for ever
>   because he delights in steadfast love.
He will again have compassion upon us,
>   he will tread our iniquities under foot.
Thou wilt cast all our sins
>   into the depths of the sea.

Micah 7:18–19, RSV

But he, desiring to justify himself, said to Jesus, "And who is my neighbor?" Jesus replied, "A man was going down from Jerusalem to Jericho and he fell among robbers, who stripped him and beat him, and departed, leaving him half dead. Now by chance a priest was going down that road; and when he saw him he passed by on the other side.

"So likewise a Levite, when he came to the place and saw him, passed by on the other side. But a Samaritan, as he journeyed, came to where he was; and when he saw him, he had compassion, and went to him and bound up his wounds, pouring on oil and wine; then he set him on his own beast and brought him to an inn, and took care of him. And the next day he took out two denarii and gave them to the innkeeper, saying, 'Take care of him; and whatever more you spend, I will repay you when I come back.' Which of these three, do you think, proved neighbor to the man who fell among the robbers?" He said, "The one who showed mercy on him." And Jesus said to him, "Go and do likewise."

Luke 10:29–37, RSV

Seeing the crowds, he went up on the mountain, and when he sat down his disciples came to him. And he opened his mouth and taught them, saying:

"Blessed are the poor in spirit, for theirs is the kingdom of heaven.

"Blessed are those who mourn, for they shall be comforted.

"Blessed are the meek, for they shall inherit the earth.

"Blessed are those who hunger and thirst for righteousness, for they shall be satisfied.

"Blessed are the merciful, for they shall obtain mercy.

"Blessed are the pure in heart, for they shall see God.

"Blessed are the peacemakers, for they shall be called sons of God.

"Blessed are those who are persecuted for righteousness' sake, for theirs is the kingdom of heaven.

"Blessed are you when men revile you and persecute you and utter all kinds of evil against you falsely on my account. Rejoice and be glad, for your reward is great in heaven, for so men persecuted the prophets who were before you.

"You are the salt of the earth; but if the salt has lost its taste, how shall its saltiness be restored? It is no longer good for anything except to be thrown out and trodden under foot by men.

"You are the light of the world. A city set on a hill cannot be hid. Nor do men light a lamp and put it under a bushel, but on a stand, and it gives light to all in the house. Let your light so shine before men, that they may see your good works and give glory to your Father who is in heaven.

"Think not that I have come to abolish the law and the prophets; I have come not to abolish them but to fulfill them. For truly, I say to you, till heaven and earth pass away, not an iota, not a dot, will pass from the law until all is accomplished. Whoever then relaxes one of the least of these commandments and teaches men so, shall be called least in the kingdom of heaven; but he who does them and teaches them shall be called great in the kingdom of heaven. For I tell you, unless your righteousness exceeds that of the scribes and Pharisees, you will never enter the kingdom of heaven.

"You have heard that it was said to the men of old, 'You shall not kill; and whoever kills shall be liable to judgment.' But I say to you that every one who is angry with his brother shall be liable to judgment; whoever insults his brother shall be liable to the council, and whoever says, 'You fool!' shall be liable to the hell of fire. So if you are offering your gift at the altar, and there remember that your brother has something against you, leave your gift there before the altar and go; first be reconciled to your brother, and then come and offer your gift. Make friends quickly with your accuser, while you are going with him to court, lest your accuser hand you over to the judge, and the judge to the guard, and you be put in prison; truly, I say to you, you will never get out till you have paid the last penny.

"You have heard that it was said, 'You shall not commit adultery.' But I say to you that every one who looks at a woman lustfully has already committed adultery with her in his heart. If your right eye causes you to sin, pluck it out and throw it away; it is better that you lose one of your members than that your whole body be thrown into hell. And if your right hand causes you to sin, cut it off and throw it away; it is better that you lose one of your members than that your whole body go into hell.

"It was also said, 'Whoever divorces his wife, let him give her a certificate of divorce.' But I say to you that every one who divorces his wife, except on the ground of unchastity, makes her an adulteress; and whoever marries a divorced woman commits adultery.

"Again you have heard that it was said to the men of old, 'You shall not swear falsely, but shall perform to the Lord what you have sworn.' But I say to you, Do not swear at all, either by heaven, for it is the throne of God, or by the earth, for it is his footstool, or by Jerusalem, for it is the city of the great King. And do not swear by your head, for you cannot make one hair white or black. Let what you say be simply 'Yes' or 'No'; anything more than this comes from evil.

"You have heard that it was said, 'An eye for an eye and a tooth for a tooth.' But I say to you, Do not resist one who is evil. But if any one strikes you on the right cheek, turn to him the other also; and if any one would sue you and take your coat, let him have your cloak as well; and if any one forces you to go one mile, go with him two miles. Give to him who begs from you, and do not refuse him who would borrow from you.

"You have heard that it was said, 'You shall love your neighbor and hate your enemy.' But I say to you, Love your enemies and pray for those who persecute you, so that you may be sons of your Father who is in heaven; for he makes his sun rise on the evil and on the good, and sends rain on the just and on the unjust. For if you love those who love you, what reward have you? Do not even the tax collectors do the same? And if you salute only your brethren, what more are you doing than others? Do not even the Gentiles do the same? You, therefore, must be perfect, as your heavenly Father is perfect.

"Beware of practicing your piety before men in order to be seen by them; for then you will have no reward from your Father who is in heaven.

"Thus, when you give alms, sound no trumpet before you, as the hypocrites do in the synagogues and in the streets, that they may be praised by men. Truly, I say to you, they have received their reward. But when you give alms, do not let your left hand know what your right hand is doing, so that your alms may be in secret; and your Father who sees in secret will reward you.

"And when you pray, you must not be like the hypocrites; for they love to stand and pray in the synagogues and at the street corners, that they may be seen by men. Truly, I say to you, they have received their reward. But when you pray, go into your room and shut the door and pray to your Father who is in secret; and your Father who sees in secret will reward you.

"And in praying do not heap up empty phrases as the Gentiles do; for they think that they will be heard for their many words. Do not be like them, for your Father knows what you need before you ask him. Pray then like this:

> Our Father who art in heaven,
> Hallowed be thy name.
> Thy kingdom come,
> They will be done,
> > On earth as it is in heaven.
> Give us this day our daily bread;
> And forgive us our debts,
> > As we also have forgiven our debtors;
> And lead us not into temptation,
> > But deliver us from evil.

"For if you forgive men their trespasses, your heavenly Father also will forgive you; but if you do not forgive men their trespasses, neither will your Father forgive your trespasses.

"And when you fast, do not look dismal, like the hypocrites, for they disfigure their faces that their fasting may be seen by men. Truly, I say to you, they have received their reward.

"But when you fast, anoint your head and wash your face, that your fasting may not be seen by men but by your Father who is in secret; and your Father who sees in secret will reward you.

"Do not lay up for yourselves treasures on earth, where moth and rust consume and where thieves break in and steal, but lay up for yourselves treasure in heaven, where neither moth nor rust consumes and where thieves do not break in and steal. For where your treasure is, there will your heart be also.

"The eye is the lamp of the body. So, if your eye is sound, your whole body will be full of light, but if your eye is not sound, your whole body will be full of darkness. If then the light in you is darkness, how great is the darkness!

"No one can serve two masters; for either he will hate the one and love the other, or he will be devoted to the one and despise the other. You cannot serve God and mammon.

"Therefore I tell you, do not be anxious about your life, what you shall eat or what you shall drink, nor about your body, what you shall put on. Is not life more than food, and the body more than clothing? Look at the birds of the air: they neither sow nor reap nor gather into barns, and yet your heavenly Father feeds them. Are you not of more value than they? And which of you by being anxious can add one cubit to his span of life? And why are you anxious about clothing? Consider the lilies of the field, how they grow; they neither toil nor spin; yet I tell you, even Solomon in all his glory was not arrayed like one of these. But if God so clothes the grass of the field, which today is alive and tomorrow is thrown into the oven, will he not much more clothe you, O men of little faith? Therefore do not be anxious, saying 'What shall we eat?' or 'What shall we drink?' or 'What shall we wear?' For the Gentiles seek all these things; and your heavenly Father knows that you need them all. But seek first his kingdom and his righteousness, and all these things shall be yours as well.

"Therefore do not be anxious about tomorrow, for tomorrow will be anxious for itself. Let the day's own trouble be sufficient for the day.

"Judge not, that you be not judged. For with the judgment you pronounce you will be judged, and the measure you give will be the measure you get. Why do you see the speck that is in your brother's eye, but do not notice the log that is in your own eye? Or how can you say to your brother, 'Let me take the speck out of your eye,' when there is the log in your own eye? You hypocrite, first take the log out of your own eye, and then you will see clearly to take the speck out of your brother's eye.

"Do not give dogs what is holy; and do not throw your pearls before swine, lest they trample them under foot, and turn to attack you.

"Ask, and it will be given you; seek, and you will find; knock, and it will be opened to you. For every one who asks receives, and he who seeks finds, and to him that knocks it will be opened. Or what man of you, if his son asks him for bread, will give him a stone? Or if he asks for a fish, will give him a serpent? If you then, who are evil, know how to give good gifts to your children, how much more will your Father who is in heaven give good things to those who ask him! So whatever you wish that men would do to you, do so to them; for this is the law and the prophets.

"Enter by the narrow gate; for the gate is wide and the way is easy, that leads to destruction, and those who enter by it are many. For the gate is narrow and the way is hard, that leads to life, and those who find it are few.

"Beware of false prophets, who come to you in sheep's clothing but inwardly are ravenous wolves. You will know them by their fruits. Are grapes gathered from thorns, or figs from thistles? So, every sound tree bears good fruit, but the bad tree bears evil fruit. A sound tree cannot bear evil fruit, nor can a bad tree bear good fruit. Every tree that does not bear good fruit is cut down and thrown into the fire. Thus you will know them by their fruits.

"Not every one who says to me, 'Lord, Lord,' shall enter the kingdom of heaven, but he who does the will of my Father who is in heaven. On that day many will say to me, 'Lord, Lord, did we not prophesy in your name, and cast out demons in your name, and do many mighty works in your name?' And then will I declare to them, 'I never knew you; depart from me, you evildoers.'

"Every one then who hears these words of mine and does them will be like a wise man who built his house upon the rock; and the rain fell, and the floods came, and the winds blew and beat upon that house, but it did not fall, because it has been founded on the rock. And every one who hears these words of mine and does not do them will be like a foolish man who built his house upon the sand; and the rain fell, and the floods came, and the winds blew and beat against that house, and it fell; and great was the fall of it."

And when Jesus finished these sayings, the crowds were astonished at his teaching, for he taught them as one who had authority, and not as their scribes.

Matthew 5, 6, & 7, RSV

THE GOLDEN RULE

All things whatsoever ye would that men should do to you, do ye even so to them.

Christian (Matthew 7:12, KJV)

Do as you would be done by.

Persian

Do not that to a neighbor which you shall take ill from him.

Greek

What you would not wish done to yourself do not unto others.

Chinese

One should seek for others the happiness one desires for oneself.

Buddhist

He sought for others the good he
desired for himself. Let him pass on.

Egyptian

Let none of you treat his brother in a
way he himself would dislike to be
treated.

Islamic

The true rule of life is to guard and
do by the things of others as they do
by their own.

Hindu

The law imprinted on the hearts of all
men is to love the members of society
as themselves.

Roman

And We Speak to God

THE PRAYER OF ST. FRANCIS

Lord,
    make me an instrument of Your peace.
    Where there is hatred let me sow love;
    Where there is injury, pardon;
    Where there is doubt, faith;
    Where there is despair, hope;
    Where there is darkness, light; and
    Where there is sadness, joy.
O divine Master,
    grant that I may not so much
    Seek to be consoled as to console;
    To be understood as to understand;
    To be loved as to love;
    For it is in giving that we receive;
    It is in pardoning that we are pardoned; and
    It is in dying that we are born to eternal life.

St. Francis of Assisi

Almighty God, Father, Son, and Spirit, who art power, wisdom, and love, inspire in us those same three things:
power to serve Thee,
wisdom to please Thee,
and love to accomplish Thy will;
power that I may do,
wisdom that I may know what to do,
and love that I may be moved to do all that is pleasing
to Thee.

Author unknown

A CHRISTIAN'S DAILY PRAYER OF THANKSGIVING

Almighty God, our loving heavenly father, through faith and the Holy Ghost, we are totally one unity with Thee.

Thou art all of us and we are a little part of Thee. Every little cell and every little vibration that sustains us is only an outward expression of Thy divine will in perfect health and harmony.

Thou art always guiding us and inspiring us to the right decisions in family matters, in business matters, in health matters, and especially in spiritual matters.

Dear God, we are deeply, deeply grateful for Thy millions of blessings and millions of miracles that surround us each day. We are especially grateful for the miracles of prayers answered. We are especially grateful for Thy healing presence, which gives us long and useful lives in which to love Thee more and more and to serve Thee better and better.

Dear God, help us to open our minds and hearts more fully to receive Thy unlimited love and wisdom and to radiate these to Thy other children on earth, especially today and all this year.

Dear God, we thank Thee for blessing and healing each of our families and friends and for helping each of us to be better and better Christians.

We thank Thee for Thy miraculous and continued blessing, guidance, and inspiration of our careers and daily work to serve others in business and churches and charities, so that all of these will be more and more in accord with Thy wishes, O Lord, not ours. We listen and obey and are grateful.

We thank Thee for our redemption and salvation and for Thy gift of the Holy Ghost, by grace, which fills us to overflowing and increasingly dominates our every thought and word and deed.

To Thee we pray, in the name of Thy beloved son, whom we adore and seek to imitate, our Savior and our God, Christ Jesus. Amen.

John Marks Templeton

God be in my head,
   and in my understanding;

God be in mine eyes,
   and in my looking;

God be in my mouth,
   and in my speaking;

God be in my heart,
   and in my thinking;

God be at mine end,
   and at my departing.

Sarum Primer

I arise today
  in the might of Heaven
  brightness of the sun
whiteness of the snow
splendour of fire
  I arise today
in the Might of God for my piloting
  Wisdom of God for my guidance
Eye of God for my foresight
Ear of God for my hearing
  I evoke therefore all these forces:
against every fierce merciless force that may
come upon my body and soul;

against incantations of false prophets;
against false laws of heresy;
against black laws of paganism;
against deceit of idolatry;
against spells of smiths and druids;
against all knowledge that is forbidden the human soul.
against poison, against burning
against drowning, against wounding,
that there may come to me a multitude of rewards.
Christ with me, Christ before me,
Christ behind me, Christ in me,
Christ under me, Christ over me.

Author unknown

Jesus, good Shepherd, they are not mine but yours,
for I am not mine but yours.
I am yours, Lord, and they are yours,
because by your widsom you have created
both them and me,
and by your death you have redeemed us.
So we are yours, good Lord, we are yours,
whom you have made with such wisdom
and bought so dearly.
Then if you commend them to me, Lord,
you do not therefore desert me or them.
You commend them to me:
I commend myself and them to you.
Yours is the flock, Lord, and yours is the shepherd.
Be Shepherd of both your flock and shepherd.

You have made an ignorant doctor, a blind leader,
an erring ruler:
teach the doctor you have established,
guide the leader you have appointed,
govern the ruler that you have approved.
I beg you,
teach me what I am to teach,
lead me in the way that I am to lead,
rule me so that I may rule others.
Or rather, teach them, and me through them,
lead them, and me with them.
rule them, and me among them.

Anselm, Archbishop of Canterbury
(1033–1109)

O Great Spirit, whose voice I hear in the woods and
whose breath gives life to all the world, hear me. I am a
man before you, one of your many children. I am small
and weak. I need your strength and wisdom. Let me walk
in beauty, and make my eyes ever behold the red and
purple sunsets. Make my hands respect the things you
have made, my ears sharp to hear your voice. Make me
wise so that I may know the things you have taught my
people, the lessons you have hid in every leaf and rock. I
seek strength, O Great Spirit of my fathers—not to be
superior to my brothers, but to be able to fight my
greatest enemy, myself.

Make me ever ready to come to you with clean hands and a straight eye, so that when life fades like a fading sunset, my spirit may come to you without shame.

Ancient Native American Prayer

PRAYER OF THE AGED NUN

Lord, thou knowest better than I know myself that I am growing older and will some day be old. Keep me from the fatal habit of thinking I must say something on every subject and on every occasion. Release me from craving to settle everybody's affairs. Make me thoughtful, but not moody; helpful, but not overbearing. With my vast store of wisdom it seems a pity not to use it all, but Thou knowest Lord that I want a few friends at the end. Keep my mind free from the recital of endless details. Give me wings to get to the point. Seal my lips on aches and pains, they are increasing and love of rehearsing them is getting sweeter as the years pass by. I dare not ask for grace enough to enjoy the tales of other pains, but help me to endure them with patience. I dare not ask for improved memory, but rather for a growing humility and a lessening cocksureness when my memory clashes with that of others. Teach me the glorious lesson that occasionally I may be mistaken. Keep me reasonably sweet. I do not wish to be a saint, some of them are so hard to live with, but a sour old person is one of the crowning works of the devil. Give me the ability to see good things in unexpected places and talents in unexpected people and give me, O Lord, the grace to tell them so.

Author unknown (17th century)

These are the gifts I ask of thee, Spirit Serene—
Strength for the daily task;
Courage to face the road;
Good cheer to help me bear the traveler's load;
And for the hours of rest that come between,
An inward joy in all things heard and seen.

These are the sins I fain would have thee take away—
Malice and cold disdain;
Hot anger, sullen hate;
Scorn of the lowly, envy of the great;
And discontent that casts a shadow gray
On all the brightness of a common day.

Henry Van Dyke

O Heavenly Father,
In the busyness of the day
we take this moment
to reflect on the many important blessings we enjoy:
Let us not take for granted
that we have food to eat
and clothes to wear,
that we live in countries
which do not fear freedom,
but instead seek to protect it . . .
That we have families to love
and who, in turn, love us.
But most of all, Lord, let us not take You for granted.
    * You sent Your own Son as a servant.
    * Likewise You give us in our roles—
      as citizens, parents, shareholders,
      and directors—many opportunities to serve others.
We pray for wisdom and love to serve in these
roles in ways which will magnify Your name.
Help us to keep alive in our hearts the words
of the Psalmist who said:
"Not to us, oh Lord, not to us, but to Thy Name give
   glory,
because of Thy loving kindness,
because of Thy truth."
We ask these things
In the name of your Son
and our Saviour, Jesus Christ. Amen.

Dr. John M. Templeton, Jr.

PRAYER CHANGES
OUR HEARTS

Dear Jesus,
Help us to spread your fragrance everywhere we go.
Flood our souls with your spirit and life.
Penetrate and possess our whole being so utterly
    that our lives may only be a radiance of yours.
Shine through us
and be so in us
that every soul we come in contact with
    may feel your presence in our soul.
Let them look up and see no longer us
but only Jesus.
Stay with us
and then we shall begin to shine as you shine,
so to shine as to be light to others.
The light, O Jesus, will be all from you.
None of it will be ours.
It will be you shining on others through us.
Let us thus praise you in the way you love best
    by shining on those around us.
Let us preach you without preaching
    not by words, but by our example
    by the catching force
    the sympathetic influence of what we do
the evident fullness of the love our hearts bear to
    you. Amen.

Mother Teresa

THE POWER OF SPIRIT

II

ONE of the most uplifting passages in the New Testament is found in St. Paul's first letter to the Corinthians;

> "When I was a child, I spake as a
> child. I understood as a child, I thought
> as a child: but when I became a man, I
> put away childish things.
> "For now we see through a glass,
> darkly; but then face to face: now I know
> in part; but then shall I know even as also I am known.
> "And now abideth faith, hope, charity,
> these three; but the greatest of these
> is charity."

> (1 Corinthians 13:11–13, KJV)

Faith, hope, and charity—we will begin this section with some of the most eloquent expressions of faith that I have been fortunate enough to encounter in a lifetime of reading and searching.

FAITH

I AM THERE

Do you need Me?

I am there.

You cannot see Me, yet I am the light you see by.

You cannot hear Me, yet I speak through your voice.

You cannot feel Me, yet I am the power at work in your
hands.

I am at work, though you do not understand My ways.

I am at work, though you do not recognize My works.

I am not strange visions. I am not mysteries.

Only in absolute stillness, beyond self, can you know Me
as I am, and then but as a feeling and a faith.

Yet I am there. Yet I hear. Yet I answer.

When you need Me, I am there.

Even if you deny Me, I am there.

Even when you feel most alone, I am there.

Even in your fears, I am there.

Even in your pain, I am there.

I am there when you pray and when you do not pray.

I am in you, and you are in Me.

Only in your mind can you feel separate from Me, for
only in your mind are the mists of "yours" and "mine."

Yet only with your mind can you know Me and
   experience Me.
Empty your heart of empty fears.
When you get yourself out of the way, I am there.
You can of yourself do nothing, but I can do all.
And I am in all.
Though you may not see the good, good is there, for I
   am there.
I am there because I have to be, because I am.
Only in Me does the world have meaning; only out of
   Me does the world take form; only because of Me does
   the world go forward.
I am the law on which the movement of the stars and the
   growth of living cells are founded.
I am the love that is the law's fulfilling. I am assurance. I
   am peace. I am oneness. I am the law that you can live
   by. I am the love that you can cling to. I am your
   assurance. I am your peace. I am one with you. I am.
Though you fail to find Me, I do not fail you.
Though your faith in Me is unsure, My faith in you never
   waivers, because I know you, because I love you.
Beloved, I am there.

James Dillet Freeman

   He whose wisdom exceeds his works, to what is he
like? To a tree whose branches are many, but whose roots
are few; and the wind comes and plucks it up and
overturns it upon its face. But he whose works exceed his
wisdom, to what is he like? To a tree whose branches are

few, but whose roots are many, so that even if all the winds in the world come and blow upon it, it cannot be stirred from its place.

I am the creature of God, and so is my fellow-man; my calling is in the town, and his in the fields; I go early to my work, and he to his; he does not boast of his labour nor I of mine; and if thou wouldst say, 'I accomplish great things and he little things,' we have learnt that whether a man accomplish great things or small, his reward is the same, if only his heart be set upon Heaven.

Talmud

All being is from God.

This is not simply an arbitrary and tendentious "religious" affirmation which in some way or other robs being of autonomy and dignity. On the contrary, the doctrine of creation is, when properly understood, that which implies the deepest respect for reality and for the being of everything that is.

The doctrine of creation is rooted not in a desperate religious attempt to account for the fact that the world exists. It is not merely an answer to the question of how things got to be what they are by pointing to God as a cause. On the contrary, the doctrine of creation as we have it in the Bible and as it has been developed in Christian theology (particularly in St. Thomas) starts not from a *question about being* but from a *direct intuition of the act of being*. Nothing could be further from a merely mechanistic and causal explanation of existence. "Creation" is then not merely a pat official answer to a religious query about our origin.

One who apprehends being as such apprehends it as an act which is utterly beyond a complete scientific explanation. To apprehend being is an act of contemplation and philosophical wisdom rather than the fruit of scientific analysis. It is in fact a gift given to few. Anyone can say: "This is a tree; that is a man." But how few are ever struck by the realization of the real import of what is really meant by "*is*?"

Sometimes it is given to children and to simple people (and the "intellectual" may indeed be an essentially simple person, contrary to all the myths about him—for only the stupid are disqualified from true simplicity) to experience a direct intuition of being. Such an intuition is simply an immediate grasp of one's own inexplicable personal reality in one's own incommunicable act of existing!

One who has experienced the baffling, humbling, and liberating clarity of this immediate sense of what it means to *be* has in that very act experienced something in the presence of God. For God is present to me in the act of my own being, an act which proceeds directly from His will and is His gift. My act of being is a direct participation in the Being of God. God is pure Being, this is to say he is the pure and infinite Act of total Reality. All other realities are simply reflections of His pure Act of Being, and participations in it granted by His free gift.

Now my existence differs from that of a stone or a vegetable—or even from that of an irrational animal.

The being that is given to me is given with certain possibilities which are not open to other beings. And the chief of these possibilities is that I am capable of increasing the intensity and the quality of my act of existence by the free response I make to life.

And here we come to the root problem of life. My being is given me not simply as an arbitrary and inscrutable affliction, but as a source of joy, growth, life, creativity, and fulfillment. But the decision to take existence only as an affliction is left to me.

Thomas Merton

If you are a disciple of the Master, it is up to you to illumine the earth. You do not have to groan over everything the world lacks; you are there to bring it what it needs. . . . There where reign hatred, malice, and discord you will put love, pardon, and peace. For lying you will bring Truth; for despair, hope; for doubt, faith; there where is sadness, you will give joy. If you are in the smallest degree the servant of God, all these virtues of light you will carry with you. Do not be frightened by a mission so vast! It is not really you who are charged with the fulfillment of it. You are only the torch-bearer. The fire, even if it burns within you, even when it burns you, is never lit by you. It uses you as it uses the oil of the lamp. You hold it, feed it, carry it around; but it is the fire that works, that gives light to the world, and to yourself at the same time. . . . Do not be the clogged lantern that chokes and smothers the light; the lamp, timid, or ashamed, hidden under a bushel; flame up and shine before men; lift high the fire of God.

Philippe Vensier

All creatures and all objects, in degree,
Are friends and patrons of humanity.
There are to whom the garden, grove and field
Perpetual lessons of forbearance yield;
Who would not lightly violate the grace
The lowliest flower possesses in its place,
Nor shorten the sweet life, too fugitive,
Which nothing less than Infinite Power could give.

William Wordsworth

CALM SOUL

Calm soul of all things! make it mine
To feel, amid the city's jar,
That there abides a peace of thine,
Man did not make, and cannot mar!

The will to neither strive nor cry,
The power to feel with others give!
Calm, calm me more! nor let me die
Before I have begun to live.

Matthew Arnold

Great spiritual truths—truths of the real life—are the same in all ages, and will come to any man and any woman who will make the conditions whereby they can

come. God speaks wherever He finds a humble listening
ear, whether it be Jew or Gentile, Hindu or Parsee,
American or East Indian, Christian or Bushman. It is the
realm of the inner life that we should wisely give more
attention to. The springs of life are all from within. We
must make the right mental condition, and we must
couple with it faith and expectancy. We should also give
sufficient time in the quiet, that we may clearly hear and
rightly interpret. The following are true today, or they
were not true when they were uttered:

"He that dwelleth in the secret place of the most High
shall abide in the shadow of the Almighty." "The Lord in
the midst of thee is mighty." "The eternal God is thy
refuge, and underneath are the everlasting arms."
"Commit thy way unto the Lord; trust also in Him and
He shall bring it to pass." "They that wait upon the Lord
shall renew their strength; they shall mount up with
wings as eagles; they shall run, and not be weary; and
they shall walk, and not faint." "Rest in the Lord and He
shall bring it to pass."

Moreover, the time will come when in the busy office
or on the noisy street you can enter into the silence
simply by drawing the mantle of your own thoughts
about you and realizing that there and everywhere the
Spirit of Infinite Life, Love, Wisdom, Peace, Power and
Plenty guide, keep, protect and lead you. This is the spirit
of continual prayer. That it is to pray without ceasing.
This it is to know and to walk with God. This it is to
find the Christ within. This is the new birth, the second
birth. First that which is natural, then that which is

spiritual. It is thus that the old man Adam is put off and the new Man Christ is put on. This it is to be saved unto life eternal, whatever one's form of belief or faith may be; for it is life eternal to know God.

Ralph Waldo Emerson

Do not stand at my grave and weep;
I am not there. I do not sleep.
I am a thousand winds that blow;
I am the diamond glints on snow.
I am the sunlight on ripened grain;
I am the gentle autumn's rain.
When you awaken in the morning's hush,
I am the swift uplifting rush
Of quiet birds in circled flight.
I am the soft star that shines at night.
Do not stand at my grave and cry.
I am not there; I did not die.

Author unknown

The foreground of life depends on the background of life. An ability to meet the challenges of life with courage, the tasks of life with strength, the sorrows of life with serenity does not just happen. A man's way of meeting life depends on what he brings with him to life.

It is the man who comes to the foreground of life with a mind and a heart and a spirit prepared by contact with God in the background of life, who is really the master of life.

It is always true that the most important part of any achievement is the part that no one sees.

William Barclay

BECAUSE HE IS LOVE

Who of us does not have times when he thinks he is not good enough to go to God for help? But God does not help me because He approves or disapproves of what I am doing.

God helps me because He is God. Because He is life. Because He is love.

God does not help me because I am good.

God helps me because He is good.

God does not help me because I deserve help, or love me because I deserve love.

Do you love only those who have no flaws? And would you think that you can love where God cannot? Love sees things perfect in spite of flaws.

I do not have to be perfect to lay hold of love's perfection.

God does not answer my prayers to reward me because I have been good or deny my prayers to punish me because I have been bad.

God does not strike a bargain.

God does not work for pay.

God gives.

God does not wait until I give myself to Him to give Himself to me. He seeks me even when I flee from Him. And whither may I flee from Him who is everywhere at hand?

God has me in His heart, whether I have Him in my heart or not.

I do not have to be the most willing for Him to choose me, or the most capable for Him to use me.

It is not only good people God has used to do His good.

It is not only brave people God has used to win His victories.

It is not only righteous people God has used to establish right.

So I hold out my heart and I pray, "God, whatever my heart may have felt, love through it."

I hold out my mind and I pray, "God, whatever my mind may have thought, think through it."

I hold out my hands and I pray, "God, whatever my hands may have done, act through them."

For I know that God does not give His strength only to the strong, or His wisdom only to the wise, or His joy only to the joyful, or His blessing only to the blest.

God does not help me because of what I am.

God helps me because of what He is.

God is love.

James Dillet Freeman

For the Christian, therefore, his civic duty is not separated from his faith: rather it is consecrated because of Christ's teaching. This is faithful citizenship. We express our faith in our social witness, not because it is the way to win the favor of God, but because no one loves God without loving men and seeking to serve them. It is not at all a question of taking party politics to the church, but rather of taking the spirit of Christ to the inspiring and uplifting of politics.

If those who enter politics go as "laborers together with God," they will accept the ethic of love as their weapon, and Christ's value of the individual as their yardstick, by which to measure their activities.

Thomas George Thomas,
Viscount Tonypandy

Do not over-plan, nor be unduly anxious. Submit all to God and obey his guiding voice implicitly. Let the prayer "Thy will be done," be a true petition of your heart. The fruit of the spirit is joy, peace, long-suffering, gentleness, goodness, faith, meekness, temperance: against such there is no law. From this sublime statement it is obvious that as you cultivate and express these qualities in your daily life, *you will be close to God* and free from the possibility of condemnation. Worry is a form of weakness, and a tacit acknowledgment of self-limitation and lack of confidence. To live a large life, you must have large stores of personal courage. The realization that *you have unlimited resources* will fortify you for the most formidable enterprises.

Grenville Kleiser

IS THERE A SANTA CLAUS?

"Dear Editor: I am 8 years old. Some of my little friends say there is no SANTA CLAUS. Papa says, 'If you see it in *The Sun* it's so. Please tell me the truth, is there a SANTA CLAUS?"

Virginia O'Hanlon
115 West Ninety-fifth Street

Virginia, your little friends are wrong. They have been affected by the skepticism of a skeptical age. They do not believe except what they see. They think that nothing can be which is not comprehensible by their little minds. All minds, Virginia, whether they be men's or children's, are little. In this great universe of ours man is a mere insect, an ant, in his intellect, as compared with the boundless world about him, as measured by the intelligence capable of grasping the whole of truth and knowledge.

Yes, Virginia, there is a Santa Claus. He exists as certainly as love and generosity and devotion exist, and you know that they abound and give to your life its highest beauty and joy. Alas! how dreary would be the world if there were no Santa Claus! It would be as dreary as if there were no Virginias. There would be no childlike faith then, no poetry, no romance to make tolerable this existence. We should have no enjoyment, except in sense and sight. The eternal light with which childhood fills the world would be extinguished.

Not believe in Santa Claus! You might as well not believe in fairies! You might get your papa to hire men to watch in all the chimneys on Christmas Eve to catch Santa Claus, but even if they did not see Santa Claus coming down, what would that prove? Nobody sees Santa Claus, but that is no sign that there is no Santa Claus. The most real things in the world are those that neither children nor men can see. Did you ever see fairies dancing on the lawn? Of course not, but that's no proof that they are not there. Nobody can conceive or imagine all the wonders there are unseen and unseeable in the world.

You tear apart the baby's rattle and see what makes the noise inside, but there is a veil covering the unseen world which not the strongest man, not even the united strength of all the strongest men that ever lived, could tear apart. Only faith, fancy, poetry, love, romance, can push aside that curtain and view and picture the supernal beauty and glory beyond.

Is it real? Ah, Virginia, in all this world there is nothing else so real and abiding.

No Santa Claus! Thank God! he lives, and he lives forever. A thousand years from now, Virginia, nay, ten times ten thousand years from now, he will continue to make glad the heart of childhood.

Francis P. Church

We link the rights of man with his nobility as a special creation of God. As Archbishop Temple wrote, "The dignity of man is that he is a child of God, capable of communion with God, the object of the love of God and destined for eternal fellowship with God."

Faith in man as a creature is the essence of democracy, but it is linked with the Christian conception of his worth and of his possibilities. Lasting faith in him is impossible on any other basis, for we just do not possess the power to be what we ought to be without God's help. There is no such creature as almighty man. He is the myth of secular society. Our faith in man is rooted in our faith in God. Everything else depends on this. Our faith in the Almighty is the central pivot around which a Christian's life revolves.

Thomas George Thomas,
Viscount Tonypandy

ETERNAL VALUES

Whatever else be lost among the years,
God still abides, and love remains the same,
And bravery will glimmer through men's tears,
And truth will keep its clean and upright name.
As long as life lasts there will ever be
Kindness and justice and high loyalty.

In a bewildered world these things will hold
The human heart from darkness and despair,
Old as the sun and the moon and stars are old,
Remaining constant, they are ever there,
Lodestars for men to steer their courses by.
The eternal things of life can never die.

Grace Noll Crowell

I knew a Christian lady who had a very heavy temporal burden. It took away her sleep and her appetite, and there was danger of her health breaking down under it. One day, when it seemed especially heavy, she noticed lying on the table near her a little tract called "Hannah's Faith." Attracted by the title, she picked it up and began to read it, little knowing, however, that it was to create a revolution in her whole experience. The story was of a poor woman who had been carried triumphantly through a life of unusual sorrow. She was giving the history of her life to a kind visitor on one occasion, and at the close the visitor said feelingly, "Oh, Hannah, I do not see how you could bear so much sorrow!" "I did not bear it," was the quick reply; "the Lord bore it for me." "Yes," said the visitor, "that is the right way. We must take our troubles to the Lord." "Yes," replied Hannah, "but we must do more than that: we must *leave* them there. Most people," she continued, "take their burdens to Him, but they bring them away with them again, and are just as worried and unhappy as ever. But I take mine, and I leave them with him, and come away and forget them. If the worry comes back, I take it to Him again; and I do this over and over, until at last I just forget I have any worries, and am in perfect rest."

My friend was very much struck with this plan, and resolved to try it. The circumstances of her life she could not alter, but she took them to the Lord, and handed them over into His management; and then she believed that He took it, and she left all the responsibility and the worry and anxiety with Him. As often as the anxieties returned, she took them back, and the result was that, although the circumstances remained unchanged, her soul was kept in perfect peace in the midst of them. She felt that she had found out a practical secret; and from that time she sought never to carry her own burdens, nor to manage her own affairs, but to hand them over, as fast as they arose, to the Divine Burden-bearer.

This same secret, also, which she had found to be so effectual in her outward life, proved to be still more effectual in her inward life, which was in truth evermore utterly unmanageable. She abandoned her whole self to the Lord, with all that she was and all that she had, and, believing that He took that which she had committed to Him, she ceased to fret and worry, and her life became all sunshine in the gladness of belonging to Him. It was a very simple secret she found out: only this, that it was possible to obey God's commandment contained in those words, "Be careful for nothing; but in everything by prayer and supplication, with thanksgiving, let your requests be made known unto God"; and that in obeying it, the result would inevitably be, according to the promise, that the "peace of God which passeth all understanding shall keep your hearts and minds through Christ Jesus."

Hannah Whitall Smith

THREE THINGS

Know this, ye restless denizens of earth,
Know this, ye seekers after joy and mirth,
Three things there are, eternal in their worth.

Love, that outreaches to the humblest things;
Work that is glad, in what it does and brings;
And faith that soars upon unwearied wings.

Divine the powers that on this trio wait.
Supreme their conquest, over Time and Fate.
Love, Work, and Faith—these three alone are great.

Ella Wheeler Wilcox

As the art of life is learned, it will be found at last that all lovely things are also necessary: the wild flower by the wayside, as well as the tended corn; and the wild birds and creatures of the forest, as well as the tended cattle: because man doth not live by bread alone, but also by the desert manna; by every wondrous word and unknowable work of God.

John Ruskin

It is generally recognized that faith is a great vital force in the conduct of human affairs. It plays an essential part in business, education, medicine, politics, science, and religion. *Faith is the master-key* to great discovery, invention, and achievement. Faith is not blindness, supposition, credulity, or ordinary belief. Belief is of the intellect, *faith is of the soul*. Faith overleaps all visible horizons. Daily you act and walk by faith rather than by sight. You are constantly exercising faith whether you are conscious of it or not. *Your life is built on faith*. The antidote for worry, fear, anxiety, doubt, discontent, and other disturbing elements is a supreme faith in God, in men, and in yourself.

Grenville Kleiser

Love Divine, all loves excelling,
  Joy of heaven, to earth come down,
Fix in us thy humble dwelling,
  All thy faithful mercies crown.
Jesus, thou art all compassion,
  Pure unbounded love thou art;
Visit us with thy salvation,
  Enter every trembling heart.

Breathe, O breathe thy loving Spirit
  Into every troubled breast,
Let us all in thee inherit,
  Let us find that second rest:
Take away our power of sinning,
  Alpha and Omega be,
End of faith as its beginning,
  Set our hearts at liberty.

Come, Almighty to deliver,
  Let us all thy life receive;
Suddenly return, and never,
  Never more thy temples leave.
Thee we would be always blessing,
  Serve thee as thy hosts above,
Pray, and praise without ceasing,
  Glory in thy perfect love.

Finish then thy New Creation,
  Pure and spotless let us be;
Let us see thy great salvation
  Perfectly restored in thee,

Changed from glory into glory
　Till in heaven we take our place,
　Till we cast our crowns before thee,
　Lost in wonder, love, and praise!

Charles Wesley

There is in man a *Higher* than Love of Happiness; he
can do without Happiness, and instead thereof find
Blessedness! Was it not to preach forth this same *Higher*
that sages and martyrs, the poet and the priest, in all
times have spoken and suffered; bearing testimony,
through life and through death, of the God-like that is in
Man, and how in the God-like only has he Strength and
Freedom? Which God-inspired Doctrine art thou also
honoured to be taught; O Heavens! and broken with
manifold merciful Afflictions, even till thou become
contrite and learn it! O thank thy Destiny for these;
thankfully bear what yet remain; thou hadst need of
them; the Self in thee needed to be annihilated. . . . Love
not Pleasure; love God. This is the Everlasting Yea,
wherein all contradiction is solved; wherein whoso walks
and works, it is well with him. . . . To the *Worship of
Sorrow,* ascribe what origin and genesis thou pleasest, has
not that Worship originated, and been generated? Is it
not *here?* Feel it in thy heart, and then say whether it is of
God! This is Belief; all else is Opinion. . . . Do the Duty
which liest nearest thee, which thou knowest to be a

Duty. The Situation that has not its Duty, its Ideal, was
never yet occupied by man. Yes here, in this poor,
miserable, hampered, despicable Actual, wherein thou
even now standest, here or nowhere is thy Ideal: work it
out therefrom; and working, believe, live, be free. The
Ideal is in thyself.

Thomas Carlyle

Miracles! Miracles! Life is a miracle! Death is a miracle!
Law is a miracle! Reality is a miracle! Illness is a miracle!
Recovery is a miracle! Everything has an existence
independent of mine. This is a miracle!

The flight of the dragonfly, the transformation of the
caterpillar, the trees clothing themselves in green verdure,
the bough on which the grey starling sits as it whispers to
my soul, the ant wriggling in the sand—everything is a
miracle. A power greater than I rules the world. I nod
approval and marvel at the ever-changing form of
changeless Nature.

Toyohiko Kagawa

O God, our help in ages past,
   Our hope for years to come,
Our shelter from the stormy blast,
   And our eternal home.

Under the shadow of thy throne
   Thy saints have dwelt secure;
Sufficient is thine arm alone,
   And our defence is sure.

Before the hills in order stood,
   Or earth received her frame,
From everlasting thou art God,
   To endless years the same.

A thousand ages in thy sight
   Are like an evening gone;
Short as the watch that ends the night
   Before the rising sun.

Time, like an ever-rolling stream,
   Bears all its sons away;
They fly, forgotten, as a dream
   Dies at the opening day.

O God, our help in ages past,
   Our hope for years to come
Be thou our guide while life shall last,
   And our eternal home. Amen.

Isaac Watts

O my brothers, God exists. There is a soul at the center
of nature and over the will of every man, so that none of
us can wrong the universe. It has so infused its strong
enchantment into nature that we prosper when we accept
its advice, and when we struggle to wound its creatures
our hands are glued to our sides, or they beat our own
breasts. The whole course of things goes to teach us faith.
We need only obey. There is guidance for each of us, and
by lowly listening we shall hear the right word.

Ralph Waldo Emerson

I speak to men who have, in their best moments at any
rate, a lofty conception of, and a reverence for, manhood
and its possibilities. Probably in the case of most of us,
our earliest awakening to a realization of the potential
grandeur of human nature was due to our being brought
into contact with developed greatness and nobility in a
historical character or a living national hero. Though
none can be so thrilled with the limitless possibilities of
life as he who has come to understand it as God purposed
it, and at least revealed it in the Man of Men, the Hero of
Heroes, Jesus Christ.

It is no lack of modesty, but rather the stirring of latent
strength, which leads the boy to turn away from the
contemplation of his choice hero to an ambitious reverie
about himself. He knows that he and his hero have a
human nature in common, he knows that Jesus Christ

presses his own victories and achievements into men of to-day, and so he aspires to be something. That is to say, having learned respect for the human nature in others, he begins to respect human nature in himself. Maybe he is restless because he is only a boy, and must wait for the powers and wisdom of manhood to come in the slow unfolding of time. Nevertheless he has learned his earliest lesson in self-respect. He realizes that life is not a toy but a force, and somewhere within him is something splendid.

Now the only man who can hope to make his life a success is he who retains (or, having lost, regains) self-respect, who finds in himself that which is real and strong and sacred, and who guards and reverences his best qualities and aspirations. If he has no respect for himself he is sure to fail in respect for others, and mischief results.

Perhaps the most fundamental feature of true manhood is veracity. Veracity means much more than truthfulness in social and business intercourse. It means that inner hatred of unreality, that aversion to trickiness which moves a man to keep his mind free from crooked thinking, and gives him courage to face things as they are. He avoids sophistry of thought, and does not clutch at every argument that makes for his own opinions or convictions, but is honest and fair toward logic even when it necessitates a change of mind. Such a man cannot fail to be true and truthful to his fellows.

Charles M. Brent

O World, thou chooseth not the better part!
It is not wisdom to be only wise,
And on the inward vision close the eyes,
But it is wisdom to believe the heart.
Columbus found a world, and had no chart,
Save one that faith deciphered in the skies
To trust the soul's invincible surmise
Was all his science and his only art.
Our knowledge is a torch of smoky pine
That lights the pathway but one step ahead
Across a void of mystery and dread.
Bid, then, the tender light of faith to shine
By which alone the mortal heart is led
Unto the thinking of the thought divine.

George Santayana

ROUGH ALTARS

And if thou wilt make me an altar of stone, thou shalt not build it of hewn stone: for if thou lift up thy tool upon it, thou hast polluted it (Exodus 20:25, KJV).

The secret of success in prayer is to be *simple, direct,* and *spontaneous.* Any kind of elaboration is sure to break the spiritual contact and result in failure. In the above text, the Israelites were told that they must not polish, or square, or otherwise elaborate their altars; they were to use just a rough and ready pile of stones.

Israel in the Bible stands for anyone who believes in God and in prayer, and so we see from this text that effective prayer is something direct and immediate.

As soon as you begin to elaborate, you are using the intellect, and with the intellect you cannot get spiritual contact. The intellect is an excellent thing within its own strictly limited sphere, but you cannot *pray* intellectually. Whenever your mental activity becomes involved, especially if you feel that you are being clever or literary, you may be enjoying yourself, but be certain that you are not praying.

If a tiger suddenly jumped in the window, you would not elaborate, or plunge into abstract metaphysical speculations, you would pray very directly, and you would probably make your demonstration.

There is a very practical lesson in this example. The reason people usually get the most remarkable answers to prayer in times of great emergency is that at such times that they are *simple, direct,* and *spontaneous.*

Emmet Fox

"Ruth," said an old high school friend who had been studying at a secular university, "you ought to lose your faith. It would do you good."

No one had ever suggested that to me before, and it took me completely by surprise. But the seed was planted and it began to bear fruit, slowly but relentlessly.

I cannot say that I became an atheist. It takes more faith to be an atheist than to believe in God. It was impossible for me to look at the heavens at night without realizing there had to be a Creator. But I could not be sure the Bible was God's message to man, and if I could not be sure of that, I could not be sure that Jesus was who He claimed to be.

I began to argue. I argued with anyone who was willing to argue. It got to where people would avoid me when confrontation was inevitable.

"Here comes Ruth," was the general opinion of my friends, "we're in for another argument."

They didn't understand: I wasn't arguing to win, I was arguing desperately to lose. I wanted them to come up with valid reasons that I was wrong and they were right.

At that time, I had been dating a senior reputed to be one of the most brilliant students on campus. It didn't take him long to realize my predicament.

"You're having problems with your faith, aren't you?" he asked one day.

"You can say that again!" I replied.

"Let's go see so-and-so," he suggested, naming a deeply spiritual professor on campus.

I objected.

"He will talk with me, and pray with me, and it could even get a little emotional. I don't want that. All I want are cold, hard facts." I wanted to go see Dr. Gordon Clark, known for his logic, his unemotional brilliance. I felt he would give me nothing but the cold, hard facts.

My friend wound up by explaining to me simply, factually, and logically why we believe the Bible is God's message to man, whom He had made—man, who had turned his back on God, for whom God felt responsible, and to whom God was reaching out.

I do not remember all the arguments. Today they seem unimportant. What I do remember is the final step. At the very end he said, "There is still the leap of faith." It was exactly what I needed: the clear, terse arguments, the merciless logic, and finally, the "leap of faith."

If God could be reached only through intellect, then where would the brain-damaged, the mentally retarded, the little child be? When Jesus put the little child in the midst of His disciples, He did not tell the little child to become like His disciples; He told the disciples to become like the little child. And some of the greatest intellects of the ages—Saint Augustine, Blaise Pascal, G. K. Chesterton, C. S. Lewis, and countless others— have all had to come the same way, in simple, childlike faith.

How like God!

Ruth Bell Graham

FROM SAINT TERESA

Let nothing disturb thee,
Nothing affright thee;
All things are passing;
God never changeth;
Patient endurance

Attaineth to all things;
Who God possesseth
In nothing is wanting;
Alone God sufficeth.

*Translated from
the Spanish by
Henry Wadsworth
Longfellow*

Some people put their trust in their wealth. Others in their beauty. Others in their intellect. Still others in their strength. But you're likely to be disappointed if you put your total trust in any of these.

The giver of each of these is God, not you. You have been given strength or beauty or intelligence in order to let you experience humility and duty. Certainly not pride. There are people who say, "I earn my money by hard work," which is true in a limited sense. But who gave them the ability to work hard?

We should realize that God is in charge. Ultimately we must call on God for solutions. His purposes are wiser than ours. Excessive worry only increases the problems, whereas prayer and thanksgiving to God for help in solving problems often lead to surprising solutions.

My mother reared my brother and me on the philosophy that only God could protect us from mistake and harm. She could not. For example, one time we were taking a canoe trip down a small and dangerous river.

We couldn't call home at sundown as planned because our canoe had sunk. Four hours after nightfall we finally hiked to a phone. Our mother promptly drove out and picked us up. She hadn't worried about us. She knew that we were children of God and that He would watch over us. There was no reason for her to worry endlessly.

Since then I have always tried to think up every possible solution to a problem and then go to sleep at night, confident that through prayer God will guide me.

John Marks Templeton

THE SUPREME FACT
OF THE UNIVERSE

The great central fact of the universe is that Spirit of Infinite Life and Power that is back of all, that animates all, that manifests itself in and through all; that self-existent principle of life from which all has come, and not only from which all has come, but from which all is continually coming. If there is an individual life, there must of necessity be an infinite source of life from which it comes. If there is a quality or a force of love, there must of necessity be an infinite source of love whence it comes. If there is wisdom, there must be the all-wise source back of it from which it springs. The same is true in regard to peace, the same in regard to power, the same in regard to what we call material things.

There is, then, this Spirit of Infinite Life and Power back of all which is the source of all. This Infinite Power is creating, working, ruling through the agency of great

immutable laws and forces that run through all the
universe, that surround us on every side. Every act of our
everyday lives is governed by these same great laws and
forces. Every flower that blooms by the wayside, springs
up, grows, blooms, fades, according to certain great
immutable laws. Every snowflake that plays between earth
and heaven, forms, falls, melts, according to certain great
unchangeable laws.

In a sense there is nothing in all the great universe but
law. If this is true there must of necessity be a force
behind it all that is the maker of these laws and a force
greater than the laws that are made. This Spirit of Infinite
Life and Power that is back of all is what I call God. I
care not what term you may use, be it Kindly Light,
Providence, the Over Soul, Omnipotence or whatever
term may be most convenient. I care not what the term
may be as long as we are agreed in regard to the great
central fact itself.

God, then, is this Infinite Spirit which fills all the
universe with Himself alone, so that all is from Him and
in Him, and there is nothing that is outside. Indeed and
in truth, then, in Him we live and move and have our
being. He is the life continually receiving our life from
Him. We are partakers of the life of God; and though we
differ from Him in that we are individualized spirits,
while He is the Infinite Spirit including us as well as all
else beside, yet *in essence the life of God and the life of man
are identically the same, and so are one.* They differ not in
essence, in quality; they differ in degree.

There have been and are highly illumined souls who
believe that we receive our life from God after the manner
of a divine inflow. And again, there have been and are

those who believe that our life is one with the life of God, and so that God and man are one. Which is right? Both are right; both are right when rightly understood.

In regard to the first: if God is the Infinite Spirit of Life back of all, whence all comes, then clearly our life as individualized spirits is continually coming from this Infinite Source by means of this divine inflow. In the second place, if our lives as individualized spirits are directly from, are parts of this Infinite Spirit of Life, then the degree of the Infinite Spirit that is manifested in the life of each must be identical in quality with that Source, the same as a drop of water taken from the ocean is, in nature, in characteristics, identical with that ocean, its source. And how could it be otherwise? The liability to misunderstanding in this latter case, however, is this: in that although the life of God and the life of man in essence are identically the same, the life of God so far transcends the life of individual man that it includes all else beside. In other words, so far as the quality of life is concerned, in essence they are the same; so far as the degree of life is concerned, they are vastly different.

In this light is it not then evident that both conceptions are true? And more, that they are one and the same? Both conceptions may be typified by one and the same illustration.

There is a reservoir in a valley which receives its supply from an inexhaustible reservoir on the mountainside. It is then true that the reservoir in the valley receives its supply by virtue of the inflow of the water from the larger reservoir on the mountainside. It is also true that the water in this smaller reservoir is in nature, in quality, in characteristics identically the same as that in the larger reservoir which is its source. The difference, however, is this: the reservoir on the mountainside, in the *amount* of its water, so far transcends the reservoir in the valley that it can supply an innumerable number of like reservoirs and still be unexhausted.

And so in the life of man. If, as I think we have already agreed, however we may differ in regard to anything else, there is this Infinite Spirit of Life back of all, the life of all, and so from which all comes, then the life of individual man, your life and mine, must come by a divine inflow from this Infinite Source. And if this is true, then the life that comes by this inflow to man is necessarily the same in essence as is this Infinite Spirit of Life. There is a difference. It is not a difference of essence. It is a difference in degree.

If this is true, does it not then follow that in the degree that man opens himself to this divine inflow does he approach to God? If so, it then necessarily follows that in the degree that he makes this approach does he take on the God powers. And if the God powers are without limit, does it not then follow that the only limitations man has are the limitations he sets on himself by virtue of not knowing himself?

Ralph Waldo Trine

The name of this infinite and inexhaustible depth and ground of all being is GOD. That depth is what the word God means. And if that word has not much meaning for you, translate it, and speak of the depths of your life, of the source of your being, or your ultimate concern, of what you take seriously without reservation. Perhaps, in order to do so, you must forget everything traditional that you have learned about God, perhaps even that word itself. For if you know that God means depth, you know much about Him. You cannot then call yourself an atheist or unbeliever. For you cannot think or say: Life has no depth! Life is shallow. Being itself is surface only. If you could say this in complete seriousness, you would be an atheist; but otherwise you are not. He who knows about depth knows about God.

Paul Tillich

Take no anxious thought for the morrow, since God supplies you now and always with everything essential to your welfare. He speaks to your consciousness, and through this direct channel supplies you with *an inexhaustible store of spiritual thoughts*. As you assimilate these ideas and apply them in your daily life, you will become more deeply conscious of your alliance with the source of all that is good, true, and eternal. When you delight to do only the will of God, and to keep His law uppermost in your heart, you will have a foretaste of heaven. *Look to God for everything.* Look upward with an earnest desire for guidance, and there will come to you a revelation and benediction from the Giver of every good and perfect gift.

Grenville Kleiser

There is hidden within the mind of man a Divinity; there is incarnated in you and me that which is an incarnation of God. This Divine Sonship is not a projection of that which is unlike our nature; it is not a projection of the Divine into the human. God cannot project Himself outside Himself; God can only express Himself within Himself. There is and can be no such thing as a distinct or separate individual that would be separate from the universe. . . . Man is not an individual *in* God, for this would presuppose isolation and separation and disunion. Man is an individualization *of* God. . . . There is no God beyond Truth, and no revelation higher than the realization of the Divinity within us.

Ernest Holmes

THE TRAVELER

He has put on invisibility.
Dear Lord, I cannot see—
But this I know, although the road ascends
And passes from my sight,
That there will be no night;
That You will take him gently by the hand
And lead him on
Along the road of life that never ends,
And he will find it is not death but dawn.
I do not doubt that You are there as here,
And you will hold him dear.

Our life did not begin with birth,
It is not of the earth;
And this that we call death, it is no more
then the opening and closing of a door—
And in Your house how many rooms must be
Beyond this one where we rest momently.

Dear Lord, I thank You for the faith that frees,
The love that knows it cannot lose its own;
The love that, looking through the shadows, sees
That You and he and I are ever one!

James Dillet Freeman

When you are in right relationship to God, all else will adjust itself correctly and harmoniously. The precise counsel is to seek first the kingdom of God and his righteousness, and all these things will be added unto you. That is to say, when you sincerely desire divine truth, and seek it with all your heart, it will answer all your questions, solve your problems, and satisfy your desires. When your life is in strict conformity to the divine plan, *you will want only what God wants you to have,* therefore you cannot possibly be disappointed. God is love, hence He wants you to have the wonderful things He has created for you, all of which are for your present good and ultimate progress into His Kingdom.

Grenville Kleiser

We must get rid of the idea that God punishes man
in any way, or that He has made saints of some and
withheld His grace from others, or that He will accede to
our wishes and change laws in order to accommodate us,
or that we are unjustly used because our poverty or
sickness has not been removed after much beseeching.
The whole order of our thinking must in this respect be
reversed. God is more willing to give than we are to
receive, and has actually placed every desire right at our
hand waiting for us to get into the proper mental attitude
to have them fulfilled, for God is not matter, nor do His
gifts consist of things made; God is Spirit, and they who
receive His gifts do so in Spirit; and through the spiritual wisdom and understanding which is poured into
the consciousness they create through mental action the
fulfillment.

Charles Fillmore

CHILDHOOD AND AGE

Our birth is but a sleep and a forgetting;
The Soul that rises with us, our life's Star,
   Hath had elsewhere its setting,
    And cometh from afar;
   Not in entire forgetfulness
   And not in utter nakedness,
But trailing clouds of glory do we come
   From God, Who is our home:
Heaven lies about us in our infancy!

Shades of the prison-house begin to close
   Upon the growing boy,
But he beholds the light, and whence it flows,
   He sees it in his joy;
The youth, who daily farther from the east
   Must travel, still is nature's priest,
   And by the vision splendid
   Is on his way attended;
At length the man perceives it die away,
And fade into the light of common day.
   O joy! that in our embers
   Is something that doth live,
   That nature yet remembers
   What was so fugitive!
The thought of our past years in me doth breed
Perpetual benediction: not indeed
For that which is most worthy to be blest—
Delight and liberty, the simple creed
Of childhood, whether busy or at rest,
Which new-fledged hope still fluttering in his
   breast:—
   Not for these I raise
   The song of thanks and praise;
   But for those obstinate questionings
   Of sense and outward things,
   Fallings from us, vanishings;
   Blank misgivings of a creature

Moving about in worlds not realised,
High instincts before which our mortal nature
Did tremble like a guilty thing surprised:
    But for those first affections,
    Those shadowy recollections,
  Which, be they what they may,
Are yet the fountain light of all our day,
Are yet a master light of all our seeing;
Uphold us, cherish, and have power to make
Our noisy years seem moments in the being
Of the eternal silence: truths that wake,
    To perish ever:
Which neither listlessness, nor mad endeavour,
    Nor man nor boy,
  Nor all that is at enmity with joy,
Can utterly abolish or destroy!
  Hence in a season of calm weather,
  Though inland far we be,
Our souls have sight of that immortal sea
  Which brought us hither,
  Can in a moment travel thither,
And see the children sport upon the shore,
And hear the mighty waters rolling evermore.

William Wordsworth

ALL THINGS BRIGHT
AND BEAUTIFUL

All things bright and beautiful,
All creatures great and small,
All things wise and wonderful:
The Lord God made them all.

Each little flower that opens,
Each little bird that sings,
He made their glowing colors,
He made their tiny wings.

The purple headed mountain,
The river running by,
The sunset and the morning
That brightens up the sky,

The cold wind in the winter
The pleasant summer sun,
The ripe fruits in the garden:
He made them every one.

He gave us eyes to see them,
And lips that we might tell
How great is God Almighty
Who has made all things well.

Cecil Frances Alexander

THANATOPSIS

So live, that when thy summons comes to join
The innumerable caravan, which moves
To that mysterious realm, where each shall take
His chamber in the silent halls of death,
Thou go, not like the quarry-slave at night,
Scourged to his dungeon, but, sustained and soothed
By an unfaltering trust, approach thy grave
Like one who wraps the drapery of his couch
About him, and lies down to pleasant dreams.

William Cullen Bryant

HOPE

Henry Thoreau, the New England philosopher, once urged his readers to "print your hopes upon your mind."

Visualize them clearly, he meant.

Don't settle for vague yearnings or fuzzy dreams.

Summon up definite pictures of hopes being realized, of dreams coming true.

Hold these pictures in your conscious mind, clear, vivid, distinct, until they sink down into your unconscious mind.

Once your unconscious mind absorbs them, it will work ceaselessly, day and night, to transform the realizable wish into a tangible reality.

You won't even have to remind it.

It will remind you.

All of us know times when the fires of hope seem to burn low. When they do, we go around expecting the worst to happen. We're afraid to attempt anything new or different because we're convinced that the chances of failure outweigh the chances of success and if nothing is going to work, if it's impossible to improve things, if the outlook is hopeless, why try?

What's the cure for this condition?

Time is one remedy. Wait a while. Hope is persistent. Sooner or later, she will come back.

Meantime, it might help to remember, when you wake up in the morning, that the world around you contains tremendous affirmations of hope:

Spring treading on winter's heels, with snowdrops and crocuses leading the way.

Summer, autumn, winter in unfailing progression.

Dawn displacing darkness, rainbows following storms, tides that always come in again, comets that return on time to the split second. No matter what happens in small human lives, the great clock of the universe still ticks.

And, on the day that's facing you, hope herself whispers that something may come along to rekindle the flame: a new friend, a new experience, a new insight. Even a new book may say: "Why are you treating hope like a stranger? Stop slamming the door in her face. Make friends with her! Invite her in!"

If you do, you can be sure of one thing.

She'll come right in.

The French novelist, Gustave Flaubert, once wrote, "The principal thing in the world is to keep the soul aloft."

What will do that?

Work won't do it, play won't do it, success won't do it, money won't do it.

Hope will do it.

Because hope gives the soul wings.

I looked up "hope" in my big dictionary this morning. "Hope," says Mr. Webster, is "desire accompanied with expectation of obtaining what is desired."

In other words, hope isn't merely wishing or wanting, hope is also expecting to receive, or achieve, or improve, or whatever. That little glow of expectation is what makes hope a more powerful attitude than merely wishing or wanting.

More and more doctors are becoming aware of this power. Medical science is finding that the attitude of the patient is just as important as the remedies or medicines administered—probably more important.

How does it work? Well, if you have a health problem and you hope, strongly and confidently, to get well, you are constantly creating the mental image of a healthy self. It's almost as if the mind says to the body, "You may be sick at the moment; nevertheless I see you as recovered in the near future." And something in the body says, "Well, if this cheerful concept of me exists, I had better make an effort to live up to it, hadn't I?" Then it proceeds to do so.

"Hope deferred," says the Bible, "maketh the heart sick."

Yes, that's true; it does.

But hope applied—ah, that may make the heart well. And the rest of the body, too.

"To be seventy years young," Oliver Wendell Holmes once remarked, "is often far more cheerful than to be forty years old."

Can growing older really be a hopeful thing?

Yes, if you can deal with a certain number of "ifs."

It can be hopeful if you believe that each age you pass through has its advantages as well as its limitations.

If you retain the capacity to welcome change, so that new ideas and new experiences do not dismay you.

If, as the years pass, you grow more skilled in your work.

If you manage to become more tolerant, more generous, more understanding where other people are concerned.

If, gradually, you come to know who you are and have the courage to be it.

Two thousand years ago Cicero said that old age is "the crown of life, our play's last act."

A hopeful thought.

But you have to work to make it come true.

James Dillet Freeman

Our work-a-day lives are filled with opportunities to bless others. The power of a single glance or an encouraging smile must never be underestimated. Several years ago I worked as a businessman in Philadelphia, Pennsylvania. Every day I rode the commuter train from my suburban home into center city. Then I walked six blocks to my place of work. One morning the newspaper carried the story of a young man who had been stopped by police just as he was about to jump off the Delaware River Bridge in a suicide attempt.

Later, when he calmed down, he told his story. He had been out of work and was despondent. In his state of despair at living in such an unfriendly and difficult world, he said to himself, "I'm going to walk down Market

Street to the bridge. If I see just one person who smiles or looks happy, I'll feel there is some hope, and I'll turn around and return home. But on that long walk down that busy street through crowds of people, I never saw one look of hope, not one smiling face."

As I read the article I wondered to myself, Was I walking on Market Street at the same time as that young man. Did we pass each other in the crowd? Was my face one of those that he looked into that morning? I will never know, but I am ever more aware of the power of a single smile, an approving nod. How many people have made a difference in our lives?

We need to ask ourselves these questions:

Who are the people in my life who inspired me, who gave me a "leg-up" when I needed it? Who encouraged me and believed in me?

Who were the persons with whom I really didn't get along, who were really quite a trial to me, but who caused me to grow, although unwillingly at the time?

Take a moment to run the movie of your life backward to your childhood. Search the scenes from home, school, neighborhood. Search your teenage years, your work years. The obvious benefactors stand out, but let us look for the lesser known, the strangers. All of these deserve our blessings and thanks. To each we say, "Thank you for being a part of my life. Thank you for living your life so as to make a difference in mine."

G. Richard Rieger

CHARITY

TAKE TIME TO BE HOLY

Take time to be holy,
Speak oft with thy Lord;
Abide in Him always,
And feed on His Word.
Make friends of God's children,
Help those who are weak,
Forgetting in nothing
His blessing to seek.
Take time to be holy,
Be calm in thy soul,
Each thought and each motive
Beneath his control;
Thus led by His Spirit,
Like Him thou shalt be;
Thy friends in thy conduct
His likeness shall see.

George C. Stebbins

TRUE LOVE

Love, to be true, must first be for our neighbor. This love will bring us to God. What our Sisters, our Brothers and our Co-Workers across the world try to do is to show this love of God by deeds. To help the poor we must get to know them. Some persons who came to help us with the problems of the refugees of Bangladesh said that they had received more than they gave to those whom they had served.

This is exactly what each of us experiences when we are in contact with the poorest of the poor. This contact is what our people need. They need our hands to serve them and our hearts to love them. Think of the loneliness of old people, without means, without love, with absolutely no one to care about them. There are many places where we can see this suffering, this hunger for love, which only you and I can satisfy.

Think of forsaken children. One day I saw a little child that would not eat; her mother had died. Then I found a Sister who looked like her mother and I told her just to play with the child, and the child's appetite returned.

Mother Teresa

Natural liking or affection for people makes it easier to be "charitable" toward them. It is, therefore, normally a duty to encourage our affections—to "like" people as much as we can (just as it is often our duty to encourage our liking for exercise or wholesome food)—not because this liking is itself the virtue of charity, but because it is a help to it. On the other hand, it is also necessary to keep a very sharp lookout for fear our liking for some one person makes us uncharitable, or even unfair, to someone else. There are even cases where our liking conflicts with our charity toward the person we like. For example, a doting mother may be tempted by natural affection to "spoil" her child; that is, to gratify her own affectionate impulses at the expense of the child's real happiness later on.

But though natural likings should normally be encouraged, it would be quite wrong to think that the way to become charitable is to sit trying to manufacture affectionate feelings. Some people are "cold" by temperament; that may be a misfortune for them, but it is no more a sin than having a bad digestion is a sin; and it does not cut them out from the chance, or excuse them from the duty, of learning charity. The rule for all of us is perfectly simple. Do not waste time bothering whether you "love" your neighbor; act as if you did. As soon as we do this, we find one of the great secrets. When you are behaving as if you loved someone you presently come to love him. If you injure someone you dislike, you will find yourself disliking him more. If you do him a good turn, you will find yourself disliking him less. There is, indeed, one exception. If you do him a good turn, not to please God and obey the law of charity, but to show him what a fine forgiving chap you are, and to put him in your debt, and then sit down to wait for his "gratitude," you will probably be disappointed. (People are not fools: they have a very quick eye for anything like showing off, or patronage.) But whenever we do good to another self,

just because it is a self, made (like us) by God, and
desiring its own happiness as we desire ours, we shall
have learned to love it a little more or, at least, to dislike
it less.

Consequently, though Christian charity sounds a very
cold thing to people whose heads are full of sentimen-
tality, and though it is quite distinct from affection, yet it
leads to affection. The difference between a Christian and
a worldly man is not that the worldly man has only
affections or "likings" and the Christian has only
"charity." The worldly man treats certain people kindly
because he "likes" them: the Christian, trying to treat
people kindly, finds himself liking more and more people
as he goes on—including people he could not even have
imagined himself liking at the beginning.

C. S. Lewis

The plain truth emerges that if a man does not find
God in his fellow men he does not find God at all.
This message lies in these three lines of poetry:
"I sought my soul, my soul I could not see;
"I sought my God, but God eluded me;
"I sought my brother—and I found all three."

William Barclay

IN SILENCE, HE HEARS US,
HE SPEAKS TO US

It is very hard to pray if one does not know how. We must help ourselves to learn.

The most important thing is silence. Souls of prayer are souls of deep silence. We cannot place ourselves directly in God's presence without imposing upon ourselves interior and exterior silence. That is why we must accustom ourselves to stillness of the soul, of the eyes, of the tongue.

God is the friend of silence. We need to find God, but we cannot find Him in noise, in excitement. See how nature, the trees, the flowers, the grass grow in deep silence. See how the stars, the moon, and the sun move in silence.

Is not our mission to bring God to the poor in the streets? Not a dead God but a living God, a God of love. The apostles said: "We will devote ourselves to prayer and to the ministry of the word."

The more we receive in our silent prayer, the more we can give in our active life. Silence gives us a new way of looking at everything. We need this silence in order to touch souls. The essential thing is not what we say but what God says to us and what He says through us.

Jesus is always waiting for us in silence. *In this silence He listens to us; it is there that He speaks to our souls.* And there, we hear His voice. Interior silence is very difficult, but we must make the effort to pray. In this we find a new energy and a real unity. God's energy becomes ours, allowing us to perform things well. There is unity of our thoughts with His thoughts, unity of our prayers with His prayers, unity of our actions with His actions, or our life with His life.

Our words are useless unless they come from the bottom of the heart. Words that do not give the light of Christ only make the darkness worse.

Make every effort to walk in the presence of God, to see God in everyone you meet, and to live your morning meditation throughout the day. In the streets in particular, radiate the joy of belonging to God, of living with Him and being His. For this reason, in the streets, in the shelters, in your work, you should always be praying with all your heart and all your soul.

Mother Teresa

THE POWER OF LOVE
III

T HE most inspiring poem I have ever read is the one that begins with the words "I am God's melody of life." What a fine expression of love and happiness it represents!

The theme of love and happiness—what they mean and how to achieve them—is also at the heart of Dr. Wayne W. Dyer's many books. He clearly describes the laws of life that lead to a joyful existence and love of self and others. Included in this section is the Chloe Robinson letter he quotes in his book *What Do You Really Want For Your Child*? It is a moving illustration of how love and happiness can fulfill our lives. The letter tells us that you cannot depend on others to "give" you happiness and love. They must grow out of yourself. It goes on to say that "our mission in life should be to be as happy and positive as we can possibly be. It is our God-given right."

LOVE

When love is truly responsible, it is one's duty to love all men. Man has no choice but to accept this duty, for when he does not, he finds his alternatives lie in loneliness, destruction and despair. To assume this responsibility is for him to become involved in delight in mystery and growth. It is to dedicate himself to the process of helping others to realize their love through him. Simply speaking, to be responsible in love is to help other men to love. To be helped toward realizing your love is to be loved by other men.

Men have been known to approach this responsibility to love from different means, but the ends are always the same, universal love. Some begin with a deep personal involvement with another individual. From this, they learn that love cannot be exclusive. They learn that if love is to grow, it will need diverse minds, innumerable individuals, and the exploration of varied paths. No one human being can afford him all of these things, so he must enlarge his love to include all mankind in his love. The more all encompassing his love, the greater his growth. The love of humanity is the natural outgrowth of love for a single individual. From one man to all men.

Leo Buscaglia

Life is short, and we have not too much time for
gladdening the lives of those who are travelling the dark
road with us. Oh, be swift to love, make haste to be kind.

Henri Frederic Amiel

The supreme work to which we need to address
ourselves in this world is to learn Love. Is life not full of
opportunities for learning Love? Every man and woman
every day has a thousand of them. The world is not a
playground; it's a schoolroom. Life is not a holiday but
an education. And the one eternal lesson for us all is *how
better we can love*. What makes a man a good athlete?
Practice. What makes a man a good artist, a good
sculptor, a good musician? Practice. What makes a man a
good linguist, a good stenographer? Practice. What makes
a man a good man? Practice. Nothing else. There is
nothing capricious about religion. We do not get the soul
in different ways, under different laws, from those in
which we get the body and the mind. If a man does not
exercise his arm he develops no biceps muscle, and if a
man does not exercise his soul he acquires no muscle in
his soul, in strength of character, no vigor of moral fiber,
nor beauty of spiritual growth. Love is not a thing of
enthusiastic emotion. It is a rich, strong, manly, vigorous
expression of the whole round Christian character—the
Christlike nature in its fullest development. And the
constituents of this great character are only to be built up
by ceaseless practice.

What was Christ doing in the carpenter's shop? Practicing. Though perfect, we read that he *learned* obedience and grew in wisdom and in favor with God. Do not quarrel therefore with your lot in life. Do not complain of its never-ceasing cares, its petty environment, the vexations you have to stand, the small and sordid souls you have to live and work with. Above all, do not resent temptation; do not be perplexed because it seems to thicken around you more and more, and ceases neither for effort nor for agony nor prayer. That is your practice. That is the practice which God appoints you; and it is having its work in making you patient and humble and generous and unselfish and kind and courteous. Do not grudge the hand that is molding the still-too-shapeless image within you. It is growing more beautiful, though you see it not, and every touch of temptation may add to its perfection. Therefore keep in the midst of life. Do not isolate yourself. Be among men, and among things, and among troubles and difficulties and obstacles. You remember Goethe's words: "Talent develops itself in solitude; character in the stream of life." Talent develops itself in solitude—the talent of prayer, of faith, of meditation, of seeing the unseen. Character grows in the stream of the world's life. That chiefly is where men are to learn love.

Henry Drummond

If a hologram is broken into a thousand pieces, the image of the whole is still visible in each. So it is with each of us. God made us in His image. His divinity is in each of us ordinary ones.

Scientists tell us that we each have almost unlimited potential, yet most of us live at a miniscule fraction of what we could produce. When we open our ordinary selves to the Spirit, to allow love to flow through us into the lives of others, we become one with the Father, and unlimited potential becomes reality.

Sue Crawford

Staggering amounts of manpower and money are devoted each year to discovering, understanding, and harnessing the forces of nature. Almost everyone agrees, however, that one of the greatest forces on earth is love. Should churches finance research into this elemental force? Should schools offer courses for credit, with homework, examinations and grades? The real wealth of a nation does not come from mineral resources but from what lies in the minds and hearts of its people.

The New Testament is full of vivid accounts of this love force, among them these passages from 1 John and Luke:

"Beloved, let us love one another for love is of God, and he who loves is born of God and knows God. He who does not love does not know God; for God is love. In this the love of God was made manifest among us, that God sent his only Son into the world, so that we might live through him. In this is love, not that we loved God but that he loved us and sent his Son to be the expiation of our sins. Beloved, if God so loved us, we also ought to love one another. No man has ever seen God; if we love one another, God abides in us and his love is perfected in us.

"By this we know that we abide in him and he in us, because he has given us of his own Spirit. And we have seen and testify that the Father has sent his Son as the Savior of the world. Whoever confesses that Jesus is the Son of God, God abides in him, and he in God. So we know and believe the love God has for us. God is love, and he who abides in love abides in God, and God abides in him. In this is love perfected with us, that we may have confidence for the day of judgment, because as he is so are we in this world. There is no fear in love, but perfect love casts out fear. For fear has to do with punishment, and he who fears is not perfected in love. We love, because he first loved us. If anyone says, 'I love God,' and hates his brother, he is a liar; for he who does not love his brother whom he has seen, cannot love God whom he has not seen. And this commandment we have from him, that he who loves God should love his brother also" (1 John 4:7–21, RSV).

"If you love those who love you, what credit is that to you? For even sinners love those who love them. And if you do good to those who do good to you, what credit is that to you? For even sinners do the same. And if you lend to those from whom you hope to receive, what credit is that to you? Even sinners lend to sinners, to receive as much again. But love your enemies, and do good, and lend, expecting nothing in return; and your reward will be great, and you will be sons of the Most High; for he is kind to the ungrateful and the selfish. Be merciful, even as your Father is merciful.

"Judge not, and you will not be judged; condemn not, and you will not be condemned; forgive, and you will be forgiven; give, and it will be given you; good measure, pressed down, shaken together, running over, will be put into your lap. For the measure you give will be the measure you get back (Luke 6:32–38, RSV).

This love force can be harnessed if we listen to our own hearts and minds, and follow its laws of life that lead to a joyous existence.

John Marks Templeton

Although Love is always what we really want, we are often afraid of Love without consciously knowing it, and so we may act both blind and deaf to Love's presence. Yet, as we help ourselves and each other let go of fear, we begin to experience a personal transformation. We start to see beyond our old reality as defined by the physical senses, and we enter a state of clarity in which we discover that all minds are joined, that we share a common Self, and that inner peace and Love are in fact all that are real.

With Love as our only reality, health and wholeness can be viewed as inner peace, and healing can be seen as letting go of fear.

Gerald G. Jampolsky

LIFE'S MIRROR

There are loyal hearts, there are spirits brave,
　　There are souls that are pure and true;
Then give to the world the best you have,
　　And the best will come back to you.

Give love, and love to your life will flow,
　　A strength in your utmost need;
Have faith, and a score of hearts will show
　　Their faith in your work and deed.

Give truth, and your gift will be paid in kind;
　　And honor will honor meet,
And the smile which is sweet will surely find
　　A smile that is just as sweet.

Give pity and sorrow to those who mourn;
　　You will gather in flowers again
The scattered seeds from your thought outborne,
　　Though the sowing seemed in vain.

For life is the mirror of king and slave;
   'Tis just what we are and do;
Then give to the world the best you have,
   And the best will come back to you.

Madeline S. Bridges

When you love yourself, you are secure and "within-dependent." You can face the changes in the world without threat. If you do not love yourself, you are not centered in the reality of yourself which *is* love. You are not letting yourself BE love. You are dependent for security on whether some other person acts lovingly toward you. In this consciousness every change in people and every changing condition is a threat that triggers in you a reaction of hate or resistance.

While riding in an elevator in a Spokane hotel, Bayard Rustin was ordered by a white man to lace up his shoes. Without objection or hesitation, he did as he was ordered. The man then handed him a tip. Rustin refused, saying, "Oh, I didn't do it for money. I assumed you really needed help." The man was extremely embarrassed and then apologetic. He invited Rustin to come to his room where they had a meaningful exchange on the subject of human relations.

You may say, "But I could never act like that!" It is not easy. It takes great inner strength which comes only from feelings of self-respect and mature self-love. The man obviously had a poor regard for himself, and that was the root of his discrimination. Rustin could treat the man lovingly without offense simply because the act of obvious discrimination was no threat to his security. He was established in the reality of his own being, which was love. Thus he could easily love his neighbor as himself, for he easily loved and respected himself.

Note that Bayard Rustin had a choice. He could have taken offense and then reacted in hostility and anger. But in that case he would have revealed a lack of self-respect. Or, as he did, he could simply *be* what he knew himself to be—a creature centered in the love of the Infinite which was adequate to help and heal any situation. No one would have criticized him if he had chosen the way of anger, for that is the way of the world. However, the wise man will always ask himself, "Why should I let another person determine how I am going to act?" The apostle Paul had often faced this kind of choice, thus it was from his own painful experience that he urged us not to let the world around us squeeze us into its own mold, but rather to let God remold our minds from within. Every one of us has a choice many times a day whether to react to situations in human consciousness, or, as Meister Eckhart might say, to let God be God in you.

Eric Butterworth

In discussing love, it would be well to consider the following premises:

One cannot give what he does not possess. To give love you must possess love.

One cannot teach what he does not understand. To teach love you must comprehend love.

One cannot know what he does not study. To study love
you must live in love.

One cannot appreciate what he does not recognize. To
recognize love you must be receptive to love.

One cannot have doubt about that which he wishes to
trust. To trust love you must be convinced of love.

One cannot admit what he does not yield to. To yield to
love you must be vulnerable to love.

One cannot live what he does not dedicate himself to. To
dedicate yourself to love you must be forever growing
in love.

Leo Buscaglia

God is love and you are made in His image. The more
love you express in your daily life, the more you reflect
God. The better you conform your mind to truth and
righteousness the nearer you live to God. The highest
happiness will come to you when you realize the
imminence of God and the all-inclusive nature of His
goodness. *Resolve this day* to keep your thoughts in
harmony with divine *love, truth and goodness*. Thus you
will steadily progress toward the better, larger, fuller life
which is your rightful heritage. God is good and God is
everywhere, hence *good is available to you always*. There can
be no better way than God's way since He is supreme.
For your highest standard of character and conduct you
must go to God.

Grenville Kleiser

HAPPINESS

Children and Grandchildren,

As the year comes to a close, I want to tell each of you how much I love you and how special you are to me.

In this existence that we call life, I have learned two things: That each of us is special and unique in the universe and that love is the most powerful device that we have in our lives.

Our contribution to this planet should be that of becoming all that we can become as a person and allowing each and every other person that same privilege. If we do this through love and caring and by being a nonjudgmental person, when we leave this place, as we all will, it will be better because of our having been here.

Our mission in life should be to be as happy and as positive as we can possibly be. It is our God-given right, and unless we are truly happy with ourselves and love ourselves as the unique and special individuals that we are, we can never totally give of ourselves to others and make this planet the beautiful, loving, and peaceful place that we would wish it to be.

Self-love is not selfish. It is the most positive and perfect way that you can thank God for your life. If you love yourself and know that you are perfect in God's eyes, then you will be able to radiate this message to others and reinforce in them that they, too, are perfect. That is the only way that everyone can achieve this elusive thing that we call happiness.

Happiness, in itself, does not exist. It is an illusion. Only by being happy with ourselves can we find it. If you search the world until you die, you will never find it. You will not find it in material things, excitement, other people, wishing for it, buying it, or by any other means. It is totally personal and comes from within.

The wonderful thing is that it is there for everyone, and no matter who you are or what your circumstances, you must realize that it is your gift. You are entitled to it, and there are no strings attached. You must never depend on another person to "give" you happiness; that places too much of a burden on both of you. If you are truly happy inside yourself and allow the other person that same right, then you automatically bring happiness to each other without even trying, and it is a bonus because it is not expected or anticipated . . . it just is.

Our responsibility to this planet, ourselves, and others is to be as positive as we can possibly be. This does not mean being unrealistic; it only means that no matter what the circumstances and how they affect us, we maintain our inner calm, our unwavering knowledge that we are unique and that there is nothing that can shake our belief in ourselves if we don't allow it to.

We must face each situation in our lives with dignity and love and allow the other person that same right.

Life is not a game of there having to be a winner and a loser. We are all winners. Only when we perceive ourselves or others as winners or losers do we place a label on something that isn't really there. Let yourself be a winner in life and allow the other person to be a winner too. In that way, everyone wins.

We are each unique from the day of birth. Small children need the protection of their parents until they are old enough to take care of themselves physically, but we should, from the day each baby is born, recognize that a baby is a human being, exactly as we are, in a tiny body. They are not "apprentice people."

Life is wonderful and beautiful; God intended it to be that way. It is only through our own attitudes about ourselves and others that we allow it to become less than perfect.

Our bodies are made up of billions of cells, and in order for us to maintain perfect health, each of these cells must operate at its optimum level. If we have sick or weak cells, then our healthy cells must work harder to counteract this negative situation so that the body as a whole can be healthy.

Our planet is like a body, and each of us is one of the cells. It is our responsibility to this body that we call our planet to be a healthy, happy cell that radiates nothing but goodness and positiveness. Only in this way can we help counteract the sick or weak cells and make our world perfect and beautiful in every way. There is no room for negative thinking and selfishness. Only by being the best that we can be, and allowing others the same right, can this be accomplished.

We must each strive to become a loving, nonjudgmental person and to give every other person, no matter how much he or she differs from us in looks, behavior, or beliefs, the right to also become a loving, nonjudgmental person. This is the only way our planet will survive.

I expect to live a long and fulfilling life and to continue to grow and learn, but if I were to be gone tomorrow, this is what I would like to leave as my message to each of you.

I love each of you and accept you exactly as you are. I want and expect nothing more from you than your right to be happy and fulfilled as a unique person. I, in turn, will try to become the very best person I can so that you will never have to look on me as a burden or feel any responsibility for me other than sharing with me your love and your self as a person if you so choose.

There is nothing that you will ever do that will disappoint me or make me love you less than I do. You have my unconditional love and the sure knowledge that this will never change. We are all on our own paths even though our lives are intertwined with each other's.

All I hope and expect from you is that you exercise your God-given right to be happy and become the very best that you can become and allow that same right to everyone else with no reservations or conditions.

Au aloha oe nui loa [I love you very much].

Chloe Robinson

Joy is prayer—Joy is strength—Joy is love—Joy is a net of love by which you can catch souls. She gives most who gives with joy.

The best way to show our gratitude to God and the people is to accept everything with joy. A joyful heart is the inevitable result of a heart burning with love.

We all long for heaven where God is but we have it in our power to be in heaven with Him right now—to be happy with Him at this very moment. But being happy with Him now means:
loving as He loves,
helping as He helps,
giving as He gives,
serving as He serves,
rescuing as He rescues,
being with Him for all the twenty-four hours,
touching Him in His distressing disguise.

Mother Teresa

Happiness sought eludes. Happiness given returns. The pursuit of happiness is never successful because happiness is always a by-product. Ralph Waldo Trine has said:

"There is no such thing as finding true happiness by searching for it directly. It must come, if it comes at all, indirectly, or by the service, the love, and the happiness we give to others. So there is no such thing as finding true greatness by searching for it directly. It always, without a single exception, has come indirectly in this same way, and it is not at all probable that this great eternal law is going to be changed to suit any particular case or cases. Then recognize it, put your life into harmony with it, and reap the reward of its observance, or fail to recognize it and pay the penalty accordingly; for the law itself will remain unchanged. Life is not, we may say, for mere passing pleasure, but for the highest unfoldment that one can attain to, the noblest character that one can render to all mankind. In this, however, we will find the highest pleasure, for in this the only real pleasure lies."

If we endorse the humble approach, we should radiate love and happiness as faithfully as the sun radiates light and warmth. As sunlight is a creative source, so can our love be a creative source of new life and ideas. God is the source of love. Love cannot flow in unless it also flows out. The Spirit of God is like a stream of water and His disciples are like many beautiful fountains fed by this river of waters. Each one of us is such a fountain, and it is our task to keep the channel open so that God's Spirit can flow through us and others can see His glory. Without God, we are not likely to bring forth any good. If we think too much of the visible world or trust in our own ability, we become like a clogged fountain. We will never learn to radiate love as long as we love ourselves, for if we are characterized by self-concern, we will radiate self-concern.

Jesus then said to His disciples, "If anyone wishes to be a follower of mine, he must leave self behind; he must take up his cross and come with me. Whoever cares for his own safety is lost; but if a man will let himself be lost for my sake, he will find his true self (Matthew 16:24–25, NEB).

God loves us all equally and unceasingly. It is His nature to do so. We should seek always to let God's love shine forth like the light inside an electric bulb illuminating all our habitation.

John Marks Templeton

The grand essentials to happiness in this life are something to do, something to love, and something to hope for.

Joseph Addison

God give me joy in the common things:
In the dawn that lures, the eve that sings.

In the new grass sparkling after rain,
In the late wind's wild and weird refrain;

In the springtime's spacious field of gold,
In the precious light by winter doled.

God give me joy in the love of friends,
In their dear home talk as summer ends;

In the songs of children, unrestrained;
In the sober wisdom age has gained.

God give me joy in the tasks that press,
In the memories that burn and bless;

In the thought that life has love to spend,
In the faith that God's at journey's end.

God give me hope for each day that springs,
God give me joy in the common things!

Thomas Curtis Clark

Happiness has no existence nor value in itself, as an object which we can pursue and attain as such. It is no more than the sign, the effect, the reward (we might say) of appropriately directed action: a by-product, as Aldous Huxley says somewhere, of effort. Modern hedonism is wrong, accordingly, in suggesting that some sort of renewal of ourselves, no matter what form it takes, is all that is needed for happiness. Something more is required, for no change brings happiness unless the way in which it is effected involves an *ascent*.

The happy man is therefore the man who, without any direct search for happiness, inevitably finds joy as an added bonus in the act of forging ahead and attaining the fullness and finality of his own self.

Pierre Teilhard de Chardin

Talk happiness. The world is sad enough
Without your woes. No path is wholly rough;
Look for the places that are smooth and clear,
And speak of those, to rest the weary ear
Of Earth, so hurt by one continuous strain
Of human discontent and grief and pain.

Talk faith. The world is better off without
Your uttered ignorance and morbid doubt.
If you have faith in God, or man, or self,
Say so. If not, push back upon the shelf
Of silence all your thoughts, till faith shall come;
No one will grieve because your lips are dumb.

Talk health. The dreary, never-changing tale
Of mortal maladies is worn and stale.
You cannot charm, or interest, or please
By harping on that minor chord, disease.
Say you are well, or all is well with you,
And God shall hear your words and make them true.

Ella Wheeler Wilcox

If we put aside pressing cares and allow the life of the universe to whisper to our hearts, living becomes pure joy. Then the heart will be detached from illusions and worldly care be overcome. Even in the midst of the most chaotic scenes there will be a stillness of the soul which is undisturbable.

Toyohiko Kagawa

Listen to the exhortation of the dawn!
Look to this day!
For it is life, the very life of life.
In its brief course lie all the
Varieties and realities of your existence.
The bliss of growth,
The glory of action,
The splendor of beauty:
For yesterday is but a dream,
And tomorrow is only a vision;

But today, well lived, makes
Every yesterday a dream of happiness,
And every tomorrow a vision of hope.
Look well therefore to this day!
Such is the salutation of the dawn.

From the Sanskrit,
Author unknown

LAWS OF THE SPIRIT

1. Happiness comes from spiritual wealth, not material wealth. Happiness is always a by-product, never a product. Happiness comes from giving, not getting. If we pursue happiness for ourselves, it will always elude us. If we try hard to bring happiness to others, we cannot stop it from coming to us also. The more we try to give it away, the more it comes back to us multiplied. If we try to grasp happiness, it always escapes us; if we try to hand it out to others, it sticks to our hands like glue.

2. The more love we give away, the more we have left. The laws of love differ from the laws of arithmetic. Love hoarded dwindles, but love given grows. If we give all our love, we will have more left than he who saves some. Giving love, not receiving, is important; but when we give with no thought of receiving, we automatically and inescapably receive abundantly. Heaven is a by-product of love. When we say "I love you," we mean that "a little of God's love flows from me to you." But, thereby, we do not love less, but more. For in flowing the quantity is magnified. God's love is infinite and is directed equally to

each person, but it seems to gain intensity when directed to sinners. This is the wonder and mystery of it, that when we love God we get an enormous increase in the quantity flowing through us to others.

3. It is better to give than to receive. Giving is a sign of psychological and spiritual maturity. There are few diseases so childish and so deadly as the "gimmies," a disease that separates us from friends and from God and that shrinks the soul. The secret of success is giving, not getting. To get joy we must give it and to keep joy we must scatter it. The greatest charity is to help a person change from being a receiver to being a giver.

4. Loneliness is the punishment for those who want to get, not give. Helping others is the cure for loneliness. If we feel lonely, we are probably self-centered. If we feel unloved, we are probably unloving. If we love only ourselves, we may be the only person to love us. Whatever we give out, we get back.

5. Thanksgiving opens the door to spiritual growth. If there is any day in our life which is not thanksgiving day, then we are not fully alive. Counting our blessings attracts blessings. Counting our blessings each morning starts a day full of blessings. Thanksgiving brings God's bounty. From gratitude comes riches—from complaints, poverty. Thankfulness opens the door to happiness. Thanksgiving causes giving. Thanksgiving puts our mind in tune with the Infinite. Continual gratitude dissolves our worries.

6. To be forgiven, we must first forgive. Forgiving brings forgiveness. Failure to forgive creates a hell for the unforgiver, not the unforgiven.

7. When Jesus was asked to name the greatest law, He said: "Thou shalt love the Lord thy God with all thy heart, and with all thy soul, and with all thy mind. This is the first and great commandment. And the second is like unto it, Thou shalt love thy neighbor as thyself. On these two commandments hang all the law and the prophets" (Matthew 22:37–40, KJV).

John Marks Templeton

The quest of happiness is a natural and worthy ambition. It is erroneous, however, to think of it as depending upon multiplied possessions, selfish indulgence, or unrestricted pleasures. In all true happiness there is a large element of self-denial, restraint, temperance, and simplicity. Prerequisites to great happiness are a clear conscience, a pure heart, and an aspiring soul. *Happiness is in reality being in harmony with God's law.* If you would be happy you must aim to live well, be grateful for your privileges, blessings, and opportunities, and regard happiness as synonymous with practical virtue. It is still true that the virtuous are wise, the wise are good, and the good are happy. *Happiness is God-made;* unhappiness is man-made.

Grenville Kleiser

Happiness is the greatest paradox in Nature. It can grow in any soil, live under any conditions. It defies environment. It comes from within; it is the revelation of the depths of the inner life as light and heat proclaim the sun from which they radiate. Happiness consists not of having, but of being; not of possessing, but of enjoying. It is the warm glow of a heart at peace with itself. A martyr at the stake may have happiness that a king on his throne might envy. Man is the creator of his own happiness; it is the aroma of a life lived in harmony with high ideals. For what a man *has,* he may be dependent on others; what he *is,* rests with him alone. What he *obtains* in life is but acquisition; what he *attains* is growth. Happiness is the soul's joy in the possession of the intangible. Absolute, perfect, continuous happiness in life is impossible for the human. It would mean the consummation of attainments, the individual consciousness of a perfectly fulfilled destiny. Happiness is paradoxical because it may coexist with trial, sorrow and poverty. It is the gladness of the heart, rising superior to all conditions. . . . Man might possess everything tangible in the world and yet not be happy, for happiness is the satisfying of the soul, not of the mind or the body.

William George Jordan

I AM GOD'S MELODY
OF LIFE

I am God's melody of life,
He sings His song through me,
I am God's rhythm and harmony,
He sings His song through me.

A song of life,
Of radiant life,
Of life so full and free.

I am God's melody of life,
He sings His song through me.

Georgiana Tree West

THE OPTIMUM
STATE OF MIND

IV

IN February 1951, my first wife died and I was left with the care of our three small children and had to learn to be both mother and father to them while trying to build a business and earn a living.

It wasn't an easy period, but, along with my abiding faith in God, there were three qualities I began to develop more fully in myself: mind power, positive thinking, and willpower. I learned to quietly release negative thoughts. I would even say to these thoughts: "I lovingly release you to the vast nothingness from whence you came."

Eight years later I married a beautiful woman and our five children now have thirteen children who are a joy to us. My wife is active in the Christian Science church, which has yielded wonderful spiritual growth and strong faith for all the family.

Mind power, positive thinking, and willpower—they will take you far on your quest for wholeness.

MIND POWER

YOU NEVER CAN TELL

You never can tell what your thoughts will do,
  In bringing you hate or love;
For thoughts are things, and their airy wings
  Are swifter than carrier doves.
They follow the law of the universe—
  Each thing must create its kind,
And they speed o'er the track to bring you back
Whatever went out from your mind.

Ella Wheeler Wilcox

Every thought you think has an influence upon your life, great or small. All the thoughts you think are of two classes: Constructive thoughts which build your powers toward useful ends, or destructive thoughts which deplete your resources. The thinking of most men is indefinite, haphazard, and negative. They are frequently controlled by environment, accidental circumstances, aimless newspaper reading, and other influences which tempt their thought away from constructive lines. You can *deliberately choose the kind of thought* you intend should govern your daily life. You can close the door of your mind against every undesirable, negative, useless thought. You can be *master of your own mind* in the degree that you really want to be.

Grenville Kleiser

Imagine if you can, a cake of ice one and one-half miles square and ninety-two million miles high. It would reach from the earth to the sun.

Scientists tell us that this gigantic cake of ice would be completely melted in thirty seconds if the full power of the sun could be focused upon it!

Mental-sunshine is powerful, too! The sunshine of faith and confidence will melt the ice of inertia and fear and bring back better times. The sunshine of understanding will melt the ice of suspicion and mistrust and erase from the earth the scourge of war. The sunshine of laughter will chase away the clouds of despair.

Mental-sunshine will cause the flowers of peace, happiness, and prosperity to grow upon the earth. Be a creator of mental-sunshine!

Author unknown

It becomes more and more apparent that health, harmony, and happiness depend primarily upon thought habits. The predisposing cause of sickness is sin, and sin is thought in action. True harmony arises from right adjustment of thought. *Happiness is the product of habitual right thinking.* You carry with you wherever you go your own thought world, wherein you determine day by day your degree of health, harmony, and happiness. Whatever your present condition or environment may be, you can perform a seeming miracle by changing your thought. Your thought world is a sacred place and your exclusive possession. Nothing can invade it without your consent. *Keep your mental kingdom holy and you will be whole.*

Grenville Kleiser

THOUGHT-MAGNETS

With each strong thought, with every earnest longing
For aught thou deemest needful to thy soul,
Invisible vast forces are set thronging
Between thee and that goal.

'Tis only when some hidden weakness alters
And changes thy desire, or makes it less,
That this mysterious army ever falters
Or stops short of success.

Thought is a magnet; and the longed-for pleasure,
Or boon, or aim, or object, is the steel
And its attainment hangs but on the measure
Of what thy soul can feel.

Ella Wheeler Wilcox

The way to health, harmony, and happiness is primarily
mental. What you regularly encourage and develop in
your mind determines your character and destiny. Hence
the vital importance of closely scrutinizing every thought
which seeks a permanent place in your mental world. For
this reason be fastidious in your choice of books, and as
far as possible confine your reading to the best authors. It
is your privilege to share in the great thoughts of the
world's great minds, and to have your life *stimulated and
ennobled* by their supreme example. Help, encouragement,
healing, and inspiration are at your ready service, but you
must appropriate them for yourself. *The infinite supply of
good* is sufficient to meet all your needs.

Grenville Kleiser

THE WAY

Life is not so complex if we do not so persistently
make it so. We accept the results or the effects; but we
concern ourselves all too little with the realm of cause.
The springs of life are all from within. Invariably it is

true—as is the inner so always and inevitably will be the outer.

There is a Divine current that will bear us with peace and safety on its bosom if we are sufficiently alert and determined to find it—and go with it. The natural, normal life is by a law divine under the guidance of the Spirit.

There is a mystic force that transcends the powers of the intellect and likewise of the body. There are certain faculties that we have that are not a part of the active thinking mind; they transcend any possible activities of the active thinking mind. Through them we have intuitions, impulses, leadings, that, instead of being merely the occasional, *should be the normal and habitual.*

They would be if we understood better the laws that pertain to them and observe them; for here, as in connection with everything in the universe and everything in human life, all is governed by law—the elemental law of cause and effect. Supreme Intelligence, Creative Power, works only through law. There is an inner spirit or guide that rules and regulates the life when the life is brought into that state or condition whereby it can make itself known and in turn dominate the life.

Jesus, Master of the laws of life, and supreme revealer of them to men, had a full and practical knowledge of it. He not only abundantly demonstrated it in His own life, but He made clear the way whereby it may become the common possession of other lives; for "Do not worry about your life" was His clear-cut and repeated command. He not only gave the injunction or command, but he demonstrated the method whereby the fears and forebodings and uncertainties of life can be displaced by a force or a power that will bring them to an end.

It was embodied in His other injunction or command that He gave utterance to so repeatedly: "Seek ye first the Kingdom of God and His righteousness and all these things shall be added to you." And by all these things, He meant all of the common needs and necessities of the daily life.

The finding of the Kingdom of God is the recognition of the indwelling Divine Life as the source and therefore as the essence of our own lives. It is the bringing of men's minds and therefore acts into harmony with the Divine will and purpose. It is the saving of men from their lower conceptions and selves, and a lifting them up to a realization of their higher selves, which as He taught, is eternally one with God, the Father; and which, when realized, lifts a man's thoughts, acts, purposes and conduct—his entire life—up to that pattern or standard.

It was not merely a poetic fancy, but the recognition of a fundamental law, as well-known laws of modern psychology and mental and spiritual science are now clearly demonstrating, that induced the Prophet to say: "And thine ears shall hear a word behind thee, saying, This is the way, walk ye in it, when ye turn to the right-hand and ye turn to the left." And again: "The Lord in the midst of thee is mighty." And still again: "He that dwelleth in the secret place of the Most High shall abide under the shadow of the Almighty."

How often do the meager accounts of the Master's life tell us of His going up to the mountain to pray—*For communion with the Father*. And then we find Him invariably down among men, always where the need for help and for human service was the greatest.

This habit of taking a little time daily, alone in the quiet, in communion with one's source, that the illumination and guidance of the Holy Spirit may become alive and active in the life, and going then about one's daily work ever open and conscious of this Divine guidance, trusting and resting in it, strengthened and sustained always by this Divine power, will bring definiteness and direction, will bring hope and courage, will bring peace and power to everyone who will heed the Master's injunction and will follow His example. These it has brought to great numbers to whom, before, life was an enigma; and this because the life had been lived entirely from the outside.

The higher forces and powers of the inner life, those of the mind and spirit, always potential within, become of actual value only as they are recognized, realized and used.

The Master's *Way of the Spirit*, the finding of the Kingdom within, leads into no blind alley. It leads out and triumphantly out onto the great plain of clear vision, of unself-centered activity, of heroic endeavor and accomplishment.

If we would spend a fraction of the time that we spend in needless anxiety, in definite constructive thought, in "silent demand," visualizing the conditions that we would have, with faith in their fulfillment, we would soon know that the Master's illustration of the carefree bird is fact and not fancy—it is, He said, what life should be.

The little time spent in the quiet day—alone with one's God—that we may make and keep our connection with the Infinite Source, our source and our life, will be a boon to any life. It will prove, if we are faithful, to be the most priceless possession that we have.

While it is impossible for anyone to make a formula for another that he should follow, the following may perchance contain some little suggestions—each must follow his or her own leading and therefore method:

My father in Heaven, Infinite Spirit of life and love and wisdom and power, in whom I live and move and have my being, whence cometh my help, manifest Thyself in me.

Help me to open myself to the highest wisdom and insight and love and power, that I may serve Thee and my fellow men, and all my fellow creatures faithfully, and that I may have the Divine guidance and care, and that all my needs be supplied.

Oh *Christ within*, enfold and lead me and reign supreme, that the One Life that is my life, I may realize and manifest evermore fully.

I am strong in the Infinite Spirit of life and love and wisdom and power. I have and shall have the Divine guidance and care; for it is the Father that worketh in me—My Father works and I work.

The following little motto—a resolve for today—may contain a little aid for the following of the *Way*:

I Am Resolved

I believe that my Brother intended that I take His teachings in the simple, frank and open manner in which he gave them, out on the hillside, by the calm blue waters of the Galilean sea and out under the stars of heaven.

I believe that He knew what He meant, and that He meant what He said, when He gave the substance of all religion and the duty of man, as love to God, and love and service for his fellow men.

I am therefore resolved at this, the beginning of another day, this fresh beginning of life, to go forth eager and happy and unafraid, in that I can come into the same filial relations of love and guidance and care with my Father in Heaven, that my Elder Brother realized and lived, and going before revealed to me.

I shall listen intently to know, and shall run with eager feet to do, my Father's will, calm and quiet within, knowing that I shall have the Divine guidance and care, and that no harm therefore shall befall me; for I am now living in God's life and there I shall live forever.

I am resolved in all human contact to meet petulance with patience, questionings with kindness, hatred with love, eager always to do the kindly deed that brings the joy of service— and that alone makes human life truly human.

I shall seek no advantage for myself to the detriment or the harm of my neighbor, knowing that it is only through the law of mutuality that I can fully enjoy what I gain—or can even be a man.

I am resolved therefore so to live this day, that when the twilight comes and the night falls, I shall be not only another day's journey nearer home, but I shall have lived a man's part and done a man's work in the world—and shall indeed deserve my Father's love and care.

Ralph Waldo Trine

To cultivate a beautiful garden you must uproot all weeds and other unlovely things. This is best done not by sitting down and studying the origin of such weeds, and ascertaining their names and number, but *by patient and diligent work* in pulling them up by the roots and ridding your garden of them forever. Likewise to cultivate a beautiful mind you must uproot and cast from you all mental weeds and other unlovely thoughts, such as pride, envy, impatience, fear, resentment, and selfishness. Then you must *plant and carefully cultivate* in your mental **garden seeds** of kindness, goodness, love, purity, humility, reverence, and righteousness. As you persevere in this work, your mind will *gradually unfold into beauty and fragrance*, and your life will be blest.

Grenville Kleiser

TWELVE THINGS TO
REMEMBER

The Value of Time
The Success of Perseverance
The Pleasure of Working
The Dignity of Simplicity
The Worth of Character
The Power of Kindness
The Influence of Example
The Obligation of Duty
The Wisdom of Economy
The Virtue of Patience
The Improvement of Talent
The Joy of Originating

Author unknown

Mental good-will is a valuable asset. People around you are quick to read your attitude of thought toward them. Inner thoughts and feelings are communicated in ways other than by the spoken word. The good thoughts you think regarding others are a silent but significant force in drawing people to you and in inspiring in them the same good thoughts toward you. *Mental good-will is reciprocal.* The good thoughts you send out to others will return to you multiplied. The quality of your thoughts determines the quality of your personal character. Let your daily aim be to have as many pleasant thoughts as possible, and as you persevere in this practice *your life will be enriched* and men will be glad to know you.

Grenville Kleiser

Cultivate flexibility of mind. Resist the tendency to want things always your own way, and to have other people necessarily conform their lives to your ideas. Good reasons unknown to you may be guiding them ultimately to the best results. Life would be monotonous if all people thought and acted precisely alike. Diversity of thought and purpose are essential to a progressive world. Will to do right yourself, but do not use your will to control and dominate others. *The habit of generous acquiesence* gives right balance to a strong-willed nature. You may have the will-power of a giant, but should not misuse it. Be kind, generous, and forgiving, since these are *qualities which link you closely to God.*

Grenville Kleiser

A workman at my farm showed me a broken metal bar. He fitted the two ends together, then subjected the joint to intense heat in the process of welding so that, as he explained, "the molecules flowed together in fusion." He told me that if he were to use a sledgehammer to hit the welded bar with force, it might break, but most likely not at the point where it had been welded. He was telling me that the metal bar could become strongest at its hitherto weakest place. A similar process of spiritual application can make a person stronger at the point of former weakness than in any other area of his nature.

Once I met a man whose explosive temper frequently overcame him. "You know, I have a wonderful wife," he told me. "I really love her. But at times she is the most exasperating person in the world. I get so mad. This anger is a funny thing. I feel it all through me. It just tears at me. I get so mad!"

"How often have you been getting as mad as that?"

"I get mad all the time," he said. "I'm a contractor and sometimes when there is a contract to be negotiated I send somebody else to do it, because so often I make a mess of it and blow the whole thing by getting mad."

"Must be pretty tough for your nice wife to have to live with it," I remarked pointedly. "Isn't it pathetic that an intelligent man should be so victimized by his emotions! You recognize that it is a weakness, do you?"

"It is my one big weakness," he answered.

"Admitting it is at least the first step toward overcoming any weakness."

"But how do I get over it?"

"Did you ever hear of Seneca?" I asked.

"No," he said. "Who is he?"

"Seneca was a philosopher in ancient Rome," I replied. "He said something about anger that would be worth its weight in gold if you could weigh a statement. He said that the greatest cure for anger is delay. When you delay, you 'cool it'; the heat goes out of it."

"O.K., I will try that delay tactic," he said. "I like that idea."

"But that alone will not do it," I went on. "You have a tremendous ability, my friend; you are a wonderful person and you have fine qualities, but you need to bring your emotion under control so that it will motivate *for* you rather than *against* you." I told him about the chief solution to all human problems: to put his life in Jesus' hands and let the tranquility of Jesus control and govern his mind. The technique of applying intense spiritual welding to his emotional nature was described.

"But getting free of a volatile temper isn't all that easy," he observed.

"Agreed," I said, "but neither is it all that hard once you make up your mind and draw upon the power of Jesus Christ."

Norman Vincent Peale

You grow your best thoughts in silence, solitude, and meditation. When you relax and think deeply, you are giving your inmost powers their best opportunity to disclose themselves. Constant action and expression are direct drafts upon your mental capital. To continue growing and accumulating useful ideas, you must have frequent times of mental relaxation, concentration and silence. Beware the modern tendency to hurry and waste. The time you give to quiet and intelligent meditation will repay you well. *Cultivate quietness, poise, and deliberateness.* It is at times of inward stillness that you can best hear the voice of God and learn His will. It is then that you most clearly realize the Divine presence and power.

Grenville Kleiser

POSITIVE THINKING

CONSIDER YOUR
GOD-GIVEN DRIVE

Again and again, first prizes don't go to the most talented man—again and again the man who wins is the one who is sure that he can! A powerful fact is this: *A great drive, a powerful determination, a consuming desire, will easily compensate for little or limited talent.*

By the standard of the Impossibility Thinker, the man who booted the longest field goal in the history of pro football, couldn't do it. But no one told him that, and he did the impossible. Most football fans know his name, Tom Demsey. He was born with only half a right foot and a deformed right arm and hand. Even though he successfully overcame his handicap and played outstanding football in high school and college, he was turned down by the professional teams. They said, "You are not professional material." He refused to accept that. He explains, "I have never learned to give up. So many times in life and in sports, I have seen things turn around because someone has persevered, someone has kept faith." He adds this word of testimony about his own family:

"My parents are blessed with this kind of faith." Finally he was taken as a player by the New Orleans Saints.

Demsey's record field goal decided a very close game between the Detroit Lions and the Saints. Just when it seemed as though the Saints had victory in their grasp, and with only eleven seconds left in the game, the Lions' kicker booted a field goal from 18 yards out and put them ahead 17–16. It looked like the game was over. In two plays the Saints took the kickoff back to their own 45 yard line. Now there were only two seconds left. The coach sent Tom into the game to attempt the longest field goal ever made. It would take a 63-yard kick to send the ball from the point of his toe across the bar between the uprights. The longest field goal that had ever been kicked in professional football up to that time had been 56 yards. Tom was so far from the goal posts that even though he was sure when he made contact with the ball that it was going straight, he wasn't sure that it had crossed the bar until the official underneath raised his arms to signal a score. The Saints had won. Tom heard someone say after the game, "Unbelievable." He just smiled, for seldom had his coaches talked to him in negatives. As Tom tells it, "They were always so busy encouraging me they simply forgot to tell me what I couldn't do!"

Robert H. Schuller

Optimism is contagious. Cheerfulness promotes health and prolongs life. The good-natured man is a constant benefactor. There is a sunshine of mind that defies and destroys doubt, disappointment, and discouragement. Good humor is a tonic for the mind and body. Laughter is medicine for the soul. The intelligent optimist diffuses hope, courage, and confidence. *Gladness is akin to goodness*. The world needs all the help you can give by way of cheerful, optimistic, inspiring thought and personal example. Avail yourself of every opportunity to say a kind word, give an assuring smile, or extend practical help that will make someone hopeful and happy. Intelligent optimism is *one of the greatest constructive powers* for inspiring men to great and noble purpose.

Grenville Kleiser

I now began to consider seriously my condition, and the circumstances I was reduced to; and I drew up the state of my affairs in writing, not so much to leave them to any that were to come after me, for I was likely to have but few heirs, as to deliver my thoughts from daily poring upon them, and afflicting my mind; and as my reason began now to master my despondency, I began to comfort myself as well as I could and to set the good against the evil, that I might have something to distinguish my case from worse, and I stated it very impartially, like debtor and creditor, the comfort I enjoyed against the miseries I suffered, thus:

Evil	Good
I am cast upon a horrible desolate island; void of all hope of recovery.	But I am alive; and not drowned, as all my ship's company was.
I am singled out and separated, as it were, from all the world, to be miserable.	But I am singled out, too, from all the ship's crew, to be spared from death; and He that miraculously saved me from death can deliver me from this condition.
I am divided from mankind, a solidarity one banished from human society.	But I am not starved, and perishing on a barren place, affording no sustenance.
I have no clothes to cover me.	But I am not in a hot climate, where if I had clothes, I could hardly wear them.
I am without defence, or means to resist any violence of man or beast.	But I am cast on an island where I see no wild beasts to hurt me, as I saw on the coast of Africa; and what if I had been shipwrecked there?

Evil	Good
I have no soul to speak to or relieve me.	But God wonderfully sent the ship in near enough to the shore, that I have got out so many necessary things as will wither supply my wants or enable me to supply myself, even as long as I live.

Upon the whole, here was an undoubted testimony that there was scarce any condition in the world so miserable but there was something negative, or something positive, to be thankful for in it: and let this stand as a direction, from the experience of the most miserable of all conditions in this world—that we may always find in it something to comfort ourselves from, and to set, in the description of good and evil, on the credit side of the account.

Daniel Defoe (from Robinson Crusoe*)*

One of the secrets of a happy life is to dwell much upon your likes and to ignore your dislikes. If your mind tends to criticism, fault-finding, and disapproval, it will readily find occasion every hour of the day. There are unfortunate temperaments which dwell habitually upon the disagreeable aspects of life. The result is a mental condition of perpetual fretfulness and unrest. It is possible for you to form the habit of directing your thoughts to *pleasant, agreeable, helpful subjects,* so that your mind will be in a uniform condition of peace, poise, and healthy optimism. As you dwell upon the best aspects of life, you will find your own life becoming happier, better, and more productive. *Dwell upon your mercies,* not upon your miseries.

Grenville Kleiser

ASK "WHAT'S RIGHT?"— INSTEAD OF ALWAYS "WHAT'S WRONG?"

Have you noticed the tendency we all have of immediately asking "What's wrong?" when some economic or political question comes up for discussion?

You can think of any number of examples:

If arguing about the general business situation, someone is sure to ask: "What's wrong with business today, anyway?"

Or, about the stock market: Brokers are asked over and over, every day—"What's wrong with the market?" Did you ever hear anyone inquire, "What's *right* with the market?"

Yet I'll venture to assert that if you ask what's right about economic trends, when you're thinking about them, you will get an entirely fresh slant on things. Your mind will travel in different channels. Try it sometime— indeed, make it a habit. It is a contrary habit much to be recommended.

The negative approach to socio-economic questions has become a fixation.

People have developed what psychologists and doctors refer to as "the depression psychosis," or the looking-for-trouble habit. Bring up almost any question—about domestic or foreign affairs—and you will hear voices at once chime in that "it won't work," "it can't be done," and so on. It reminds one of the horse-and-buggy days when Henry Ford and the other horseless-carriage inventors were scoffed at.

This reminds me of an interesting example of thinking right which is related in the book *Watch Your Margin*. A smart investor was riding in one of the early two-lungers, and after a speedy fifteen-miles-an-hour spin inquired what made the contraption run. When told it was gasoline, he at once bought himself a bundle of Mr. Rockefeller's certificates. He knew that Standard Oil would sell its product and stay in business, and he also figured a lot of the early-bird manufacturers of autos would drop by the wayside. So, by asking himself what was right about the gas buggies—and not worrying about what was wrong—he made a future killing.

It seems to me that if we are to ride through the next decade without losing our sense of balance—and are to enjoy any sort of contentment in life—we need to dwarf our troubles and magnify our blessings.

If we start asking "What's right?" about this or that question we shall find we are actually changing our whole method of thinking. Heaven knows we don't enjoy figuring the fiendish taxes of today, but it wasn't so long ago that you and I both probably were thinking that *anything,* even killing taxes, would·be better than a run-away inflation. Obviously, I'll agree that taxes can be too high (they are now, from an economic standpoint) but perhaps if students concentrated on what is the *right* amount we might solve the problem.

Humphrey B. Neill

Be done with the past, save where it serves to inspire you to greater and nobler effort. Be done with regrets over vanished opportunities, seeming failures, and bitter disappointments, except insofar as they warn and safeguard you against their repetition. Be done with the "might have been," and think of the "shall be." In all development, physical or mental, there are progressive stages, and what seemed to you failures, obstacles, and disappointments, were probably disguised opportunities for your ultimate good and advantage. Let your motto be to look ever ahead, *expectant of great things yet to come.* Trust God that no good is ever lost or withheld. Direct your best impulses and inspirations to worthy work, with the assurance that *all will be well with you.*

Grenville Kleiser

There is one thing you can be most certain of, and that is that law in some form or other guides and governs every aspect of your experience just as it does everything else in the universe. Fundamentally, the universe operates as a unity, not a chaos, and the laws that establish and maintain this unity are not in conflict with one another.

The creative action of infinite Intelligence is explained in terms of Law, and the operation of this Law is of necessity in conformity with Its nature, not contrary to It. So you can come to discover that it does not matter what your experience may be, whether you are concerned with your health, success, affairs, or relationships, there is a Law of Mind at work. But the *way* It works in and through your experience you determine. Things just do not happen haphazardly, without any determining factor. There is always a cause and effect, an initial act of creativity and the manifest result.

Perhaps you have been prone to think that law is operative in some things and not in others—that there is a law relative to the action of electricity but no law that applies to your relationships with others. Or that law may apply to the positions the planets hold around the sun, but law does not enter into the question as to whether you are sick or well.

Whether you fully recognize it or not, law functions in everything you are, do, and experience. There is no avoiding or escaping its action. But it must always be remembered that law is impersonal. It is never concerned about whether or not you recognize it, nor is it the least bit interested in how you use it.

This definitely indicates that there is nothing in the nature of things that is intrinsically against your welfare or well-being. There is nothing in the universe that decrees that you shall be sick, poor, or unhappy. It would be impossible for a universe that manifests through law and order to declare that one individual shall enjoy life and another not. Neither would it be possible for the creative Intelligence in and back of all things to give an abundance of all things to one part of Its creation and deprive another part.

So it would appear that if in any respect Life seems to be withholding something from you, it is not the result of the action of Life Itself, but the result of your relationship to Life. All of Life is available to you, but the question that arises is: how much of It are you availing yourself of?

Any law, in any sphere of activity, improperly used will bring improper results. In the physical world scientists are able to avail themselves of the power of nature only when they are able to ascertain the laws of its action and properly use them. You are in much the same position. You have to discover for yourself the nature of the spiritual Law which governs your experiences in living, and then properly apply It.

Where previously you may have been using the action of the Law of Mind erratically, with the result that you felt you had to wage a solitary battle against the universe, you will find that the proper use of the creative power of your thought, and its immutable action through Law, will align your life in harmony with the beneficial nature of God.

When you properly understand this you will find that Life is for you; then you can avail yourself of all Its good in your life. You use the Law for your benefit. It is futile to battle against Its action; you direct Its action in the manner you desire.

Your ability to direct this action resides in the nature of the God-given creative power of your own thought.

When you stop battling life, stop feeling that everything is against you, and become aware of the fact that the only thing against you is your own thinking, then you start to cooperate with the great Law of the universe and through a change in the pattern of your thinking you will be able to make your life a joyous adventure in which you will encounter only good.

Regardless of how much misdirection you may have given the Law in the past, it is never too late to start to use It in a new and better way. The Law knows only to act, to respond to your thought. Your every thought is the start of a new causative action which will become manifest in your experience. And the wonderful thing is that this new action can transform and transcend any present undesirable condition in your life.

Willis Kinnear

WILLPOWER

_____

NEVER GIVE UP

"The news I have for you is not good." The doctor's face was grim as he faced thirty-two-year-old Pat Nordberg. Her husband, Olie, gripped her hand.

"Go on, doctor," she said.

"You have an aneurysm in the most inaccessible part of your brain. Your condition will get no better. You could die anytime. You might be lucky and live if nothing is done about it."

The doctor continued with his cold, factual report:

"Surgery? I'd say there's a 10 percent survival possiblity—that's all. We would have to lift your brain out of its case. I would actually have to hold it in my hands. We just don't know what that would do to your mental functioning—if you lived through it."

Numb with shock, Olie and Pat walked in a daze to the parking lot—speechless love flowed from heart to heart as they drove home.

"Mommy, Mommy," their five-year-old boy cried as he ran into the waiting, warm embrace of his beautiful mother. It was her son and her husband that made the decision so hard. Should she choose surgery with only a one to ten survival possiblity? Should she let things go, hope and pray that the next headache would never come? She remembered the first one some months before. She felt the blood vessel break. She felt the warm liquid flow around her brain under her skull before she passed out.

New X-rays were taken. The diagnosis was the same as before. The aneurysm was still there.

"Well, Pat," the doctor said, "it's a big one. If it goes, you're finished." He explained, "An aneurysm is a weak bulge in a blood vessel—we never know when it will blow."

"Why me? What have I done? I've been a good person." Self-pity was mixed with anger as Pat wept alone in her bedroom. Miles away at his office desk, Olie, a brilliant Harvard Business School graduate, prayed for guidance between telephone calls from customers who were terribly upset about their "enormous problems."

"Seek ye first the Kingdom of God." The words came from nowhere into Pat's mind. Like sweet music that comes on, suddenly sending a soft mood into a room, so the coming of this Bible verse brought divine peace to the red-eyed woman. She now knew beyond a shadow of a doubt what she would do.

She called Olie. "Honey, I am no longer afraid. I know that if I die, God will have someone better than me to love my son and my husband." She paused, and with utter calmness coolly said, "Olie, I'm going to call the doctor and give him my decision—operate."

"Pat's going to have surgery. She's going in tomorrow morning." Pat's next-door neighbor was spreading the word from house to house on their street in Fullerton, California. "Olie's driving her to the hospital on the way to his office—they don't give her much chance of ever coming back alive or with a normal mind, but she says this is the decision God led her to take."

The next morning a pall settled over the kitchens in houses on the street. Children ran to school, husbands went to work, but the women in each house watched their clocks carefully. Olie would be leaving his house at exactly eight o'clock. One neighbor called the others and said, "Let's all step out on our front steps and wave to her as she leaves—and throw a prayer with a smile and a kiss!"

Quietly, cool and calm, Pat entered the car as Olie carried her small overnight suitcase. He opened the garage door and backed out into the street. Pat saw them, her neighbor ladies, all up and down the block, on both sides. She smiled.

In the way a child makes a jack-o-lantern, cutting a doorway out of the top of the pumpkin, so the top of Pat's skull, with saw and drill, was cut out and lifted up—exposing the brain. Reaching into the cranial cavity, the doctor took the young mother's brain in his rubber-gloved hand and removed the weak section of the major blood vessel that was threatening to blow out. Delicately, gently, tenderly—with a touch of almost reverence, he placed the brain back into its place and prepared to close the door on his job.

Like the cut-out top of the jack-o-lantern, the cut-out section of the skull was now put back in place, and a protective metal plate placed over it. The entire skin of the scalp, peeled away for the surgery, could now be rolled back and sewed up. Hair would grow back in time—if she'd live.

To her waiting husband the surgery lasted an eternity. "Was she still alive? Would she ever know him again if she survived? Would she be a vegetable? A maniac? Or childish? Or—please God, the same Pat I've loved?" These questions raced through his mind as he prayed with a wet face resting down on his open palms.

"Mr. Nordberg?" The doctor's familiar voice brought him to his feet. He faced the somber surgeon. "It's all over now, Olie," the doctor said. "All we can do now is wait—and pray. It may be days before we'll know whether she is going to live and what her condition will be after that." It was the best Olie could hope for.

Her shaven head, wrapped in a white bandage, still and unmoving in the center of the pillow, gave her a deathly appearance. Round the clock, hour after hour, day after day, nurses on duty for twenty-four hours waited, hoping for a sign of consciousness. Would her eyes open? Would her lips move? Would she be able to speak?

On the morning of the fourth day following surgery, the special nurse on duty had turned her back for a moment when she heard a low but clear voice behind her. "Could you bring me some lipstick please, nurse." Whirling, she looked at Pat, whose eyes were open and alert, and the nurse thought, mentally healthy enough to want to look pretty.

If only the sentences had kept coming so clearly. Over the next few weeks Pat's wounded brain was unable to sustain normal speech. Words got mixed up and out of proper sequence. To compound the problem her body was poorly coordinated. Would she ever be able to live a normal life?

Months passed. She was able to ride with her family to church again.

"Pat," a church member stopped her, "I think you could help as a volunteer in the church school for retarded children. We need one adult to watch and observe each teachable child—would you try to help, please?" Pat didn't need to be asked twice! Here was a chance to prove that, although her speech and body movements were not functioning properly, she could still be helpful. The events that now occurred changed her life.

As Pat tells it, "I noticed an eight-year-old girl, Janine, who had no adult volunteer to supervise her. When I asked about her I was told, 'She is only a vegetable. She has no possibility for ever developing. She doesn't even know her mother. She cannot and probably never will walk.' I felt so sorry for her," Pat recalls. "I sat on the floor close to her. All she did was tear paper and flutter her mumbling lips with a finger. It was so sad. I watched her. Then when her eyes looked up at me, I smiled. She stared back at my smile—and a miracle happened. She crawled over and buried her head in my lap and sobbed and sobbed. As I tenderly stroked her back, she wet my dress with her tears. 'Oh God,' I prayed, 'if love alone will do this to a child what would love plus an education do?' I decided then and there I'd become a child psychologist."

Pat now knew the person she wanted to be. Incredible hurdles and barriers were in the road ahead. Before she could enroll in college she would have to solve the transportation problem. The only way to get to classes would be by car. And she had never learned to drive. In her present condition she lacked the physical coordination to pass a driver's test! A bright idea occurred to her. She had heard that Hawaiian dancing was helpful in learning bodily coordination. She decided to take lessons. Two years of continuous and strenuous hula lessons did it. Her body was now in almost perfect condition. She passed her driver's test. Problem number one was now solved.

She enrolled in California State College in Fullerton, California—only to be placed on academic probation. Her wounded mind could not recall what it would read in the textbook. She would read it again! And underline it! And write notes on paper! And memorize the notes! During that early period of college work she averaged only three hours of sleep each night, yet came up with only a C average. But she would not give up. Year after year after year she added units toward a degree.

Thirteen years after surgery she completed her last semester of classroom work, with a high grade point average! Her speech was now perfect. By trial and error she invented techniques to correct her language problem. Drawing from this experience in overcoming her own aphasic condition, she wrote her master's thesis, "Exercises that Parents of Aphasic Children Can Use to Teach Their Children Self-Improvement."

"Dr. Schuller," said Pat, running up to me after a church service one day, "Guess what?—I got it. My master's degree. And I'm going to work with exceptional children in the public schools. God did it. I know it. I felt Him driving me, urging me, pushing me on. My God can do anything."

Pat is now a practicing psychologist.

Robert H. Schuller

Arise early, serve God devoutly, and the world busily.

Do thy work wisely, give thine alms secretly; go thy way
gravely.

Answer the people demurely, go to thy meat appetitely.

Sit thereat discretely, arise temperately.

Go to thy supper soberly, and to thy bed merrily.

Be in thine inn jocundly.

Please thy love duly, and sleep surely.

St. Sulpicius

Lean on thyself until thy strength is tried;
Then ask God's help; it will not be denied.

Use thine own sight to see the way to go;
When darkness falls ask God the path to show.

Think for thyself and reason out thy plan;
God has his work and thou has thine, oh, man.

Exert thy will and use it for control;
God gave thee jurisdiction of thy soul.

All thine immortal powers bring into play;
Think, act, strive, reason, then look up and pray.

Ella Wheeler Wilcox

Never send a letter written in anger or resentment. If you write such a letter in order to relieve your pent-up feelings, or to express righteous indignation, put it in your desk for twenty-four hours, and upon deliberate reflection you will destroy it. *Anger in any form is weakness*, but put in writing it remains on record to stand forth an accusing witness against your better self. Resolve never under any circumstances to write an unkind or ill-tempered letter, nor to place on record anything which you could by any possibility live to regret. Make it a rule *never to say anything in anger*. Boys draw in their kites at will, but you cannot annul the spoken word. *Think well before you speak*.

Grenville Kleiser

Trouble is no disaster when we know we can manage it. Indeed, the joy of Jesus came not from the absence of difficulty, but from a conviction of power to triumph. What a day it is for a boy learning to swim when he comes up from a dunking with a sputtering shout: "Look, Dad, I'm swimming!" It isn't the absence of problems that brings joy to a man struggling to build a little business on Main Street; it is the grateful assurance of capacity for victory affirmed in the gleeful word to his wife: "Honey, we're solvent."

What brings joy to the morning isn't the thought that today will be free from problems, or difficulties or troubles, but rather the knowledge that "I can do all things in him who strengthens me." A man I know in the hospital understands that. He is a tonic when I see him, snared as he is with arthritis and a bad heart. He greets me with a grin that stretches from ear to ear and even when he feels the worst he has some cheerful word. He knows from long years of comradeship with God that he is spiritually adequate for anything that may come.

Harold Blake Walker

BUILDING ON
DREAMS
——
V

I N my teenage years, like other young men the world over, I was inspired by the courage and vision of Rudyard Kipling's poem "If." It taught me to dream—but also to be master of my dreams, and to think without letting thoughts become an end in themselves. I learned from Kipling that the earth belongs to us all and that, with courage and enthusiasm, progess is certain to follow. The final stanza of "If" still rings in my ears:

> *If you can fill the unforgiving minute*
> *With sixty seconds' worth of distance run,*
> *Yours is the Earth and everything that's in it,*
> *And—which is more—you'll be a Man, my son!*

Also in my teenage years, at fourteen, I memorized Longfellow's "Psalm of Life." It has encouraged me to use to the limit any gifts God may have given me.

We have to have the courage to try new experiences and the enthusiasm to carry them out. The result? Courage plus enthusiasm equals progress.

COURAGE

IF

If you can keep your head when all about you
   Are losing theirs and blaming it on you,
If you can trust yourself when all men doubt you,
   But make allowances for their doubting too;
If you can wait and not be tired by waiting,
   Or being lied about, don't deal in lies,
Or being hated, don't give way to hating,
   And yet don't look too good, nor talk too wise:

If you can dream—and not make dreams your master;
   If you can think—and not make thoughts your
   aim;
If you can meet with Triumph and Disaster
   And treat those two imposters just the same;
If you can bear to hear the truth you've spoken
   Twisted by knaves to make a trap for fools,
Or watch the things you gave your life to, broken,
   And stoop and build 'em up with worn-out tools:

If you can make one heap of all your winnings
   And risk it on one turn of pitch-and-toss,
And lose, and start again at your beginnings
   And never breathe a word about your loss;

If you can force your heart and nerve and sinew
   To serve your turn long after they are gone,
And so hold on when there is nothing in you
   Except the will which says to them: "Hold on!"

If you can talk with crowds and keep your virtue,
   Or walk with Kings—nor lose the common touch,
If neither foes nor loving friends can hurt you,
   If all men count with you, but none too much;

If you can fill the unforgiving minute
   With sixty seconds' worth of distance run,
Yours is the Earth and everything that's in it,
   And—which is more—you'll be a Man, my son!

Rudyard Kipling

My message to you is to be courageous. I have lived a long time. I have seen history repeat itself again and again. I have seen many depressions in business. Always America has come out stronger and more prosperous. Be as brave as your fathers before you. Have faith—go forward.

Thomas A. Edison

Only those are fit to live who do not fear to die; and
none are fit to die who have shrunk from the joy of life
and the duty of life. Both life and death are part of the
same Great Adventure. Never yet was worthy adventure
worthily carried through by the man who put his
personal safety first. Never yet was a country worth living
in unless its sons and daughters were of that stern stuff
which bade them die for it at need; and never yet was a
country worth dying for unless its sons and daughters
thought of life, not as something concerned only with the
selfish evanescence of the individual, but as a link in the
great chain of creation and causation, so that each person
is seen in his true relations as an essential part of the
whole, whose life must be made to serve the larger and
continuing life of the whole. Therefore it is, that the man
who is not willing to die, and the woman who is not
willing to send her man to die, in a war for a great cause,
are not worthy to live. Therefore, it is that the man and
the woman who in peacetime fear or ignore the primary
and vital duties and the high happiness of family life, who
dare not beget and bear and rear the life that is to last
when they are in their graves, have broken the chain of
creation, and have shown that they are unfit for
companionship with the souls ready for the Great
Adventure.

Theodore Roosevelt

PROBLEM SOLVING

One spring evening the telephone rang in my home. "Are you the Dr. Schuller who wrote *Move Ahead with Possibility Thinking?*" a youthful voice asked. I admitted I was.

"I've got to see you," she said. "I want to find out if you're a phony or not."

Amazed at such direct frankness and realizing that my integrity was being challenged, I told her, "OK—be in my office tomorrow morning. Just drop in and I'll see you between appointments."

The next morning my secretary whispered over the intercom, "There's a young lady here, Miss Barbara Bassinger, who wants to see you. She said she spoke to you last night and you told her to come in."

"That's right. Send her in."

The door opened to the amazing sight of the strangest contraption I'd ever seen. Sitting in a wheelchair was a young girl surrounded by an incredible assemblage of metal and leather. A network of steel and leather straps started at her feet, crisscrossed at her ankles, and were connected to braces hinged at the knees. These were joined to metal straps along both of her thighs, which were bolted to an abdominal metal body belt. Two black shining eyes peered at me out of a mask also made of leather and steel. She raised a hand and I saw that metal braces supported both of her arms.

"Surprised?" she said with a laughing voice.

"I must admit I've never seen anything like it before," I answered.

"I'm a cerebral palsied quadraplegic," she explained. "When I was a child the experts told my parents that I would never walk and I'd never be able to get very far in school. I grew up believing that also until I heard the words, 'If you have faith as a grain of mustard seed, you will say to your mountain "move," and nothing will be impossible to you.' I found a doctor who was a Positive Thinking expert and asked him, 'Can't you devise something that will help me to walk?' Before he could answer I told him, 'If you put an iron brace around my ankles, then my legs won't fly around. And if you stretch my head with a neck brace, and hold it steady with iron bars bolted to a chest plate, and if you put iron braces between my arms to keep them from flying around . . .' He listened to me, and this is what he came up with. I thought you'd like to see it."

I was stunned. I felt pity flow through me toward her until she started talking again, "Now, Dr. Schuller, here is the good news. I CAN WALK!" And with a creak of leather and the clatter of iron, she rose from her wheelchair and walked around the room. Then she dropped back into her chair and proudly announced, "And I just got my M.A. degree from San Diego State College."

Look around you and you'll find someone you know, or have heard of, who is a great Possibility Thinker. Latch on to that person or his inspiring story when you are up against what might seem to be insufferable odds.

Robert H. Schuller

It is easier to pluck a thistle than it is to plant a flower. All I ask of those who knew me best is to remember that I plucked a thistle and planted a flower wherever the flower would grow.

In my youth I was fortunate in having a loving mother, a kind and considerate father who instilled into my young mind that I would pass through this world but once and if I were permitted to complete my life's journey, the road to happiness would not be found through the primrose path by the easiest way but like the Christian in Pilgrim's Progress, I must fortify myself with courage and self-sacrifice to pass through the Slough of Despond in order to reach the mountain peaks of Hope and Happiness.

So, all my life, I have tried to pluck a thistle and plant a flower wherever the flower would grow with the thought in mind that to live in the hearts of those we leave behind is not to die.

Abraham Lincoln

PIKE'S PEAK OR BUST!

There is no condition that cannot be overcome with sufficient spiritual power. There is no problem that can present itself to the mind of man which cannot be solved with enough spiritual understanding. The very fact that man can become conscious of a problem at all is a proof that he can find a solution. We are here on the earth to solve these very problems, because in solving them we develop our own spiritual faculties. Every difficulty that comes into your life, every problem that presents itself to you, means that here is a point at which your are to learn something.

Do not be an idolater and worship difficulties, as many people do. When you say that some trouble is insurmountable, or that a problem is insoluble, you are an idolater and you are denying your own divine selfhood. Let nothing intimidate you. As the expression of God you are more than equal to anything that may arise, if only you have *courage* and *faith*.

Most heathen countries have a "holy mountain." This really means that coming upon a particularly high and inaccessible locality, the people lost their courage, allowed themselves to be overawed, and, instead of tackling and conquering the difficulty, they fell on their knees in abject terror and rubbed their foreheads on the ground, saying, "Oh holy mountain, do not hurt us."

In America we have no holy mountains of this kind. It is not our *custom* to grovel before difficulties, but to conquer them. Coming upon a fifteen-thousand-foot mountain, the western pioneers did no groveling. Instead, they said, *Pike's Peak or bust,* and they got to the top of the mountain and conquered it, instead of letting the mountain conquer them. To do this is to glorify God, instead of lapsing into idolotry.

Do not have any holy mountains in your life. Do not allow any difficulty, no matter what it is, to scare you. Say *"Pike's Peak or bust,"* and go at it and conquer it.

The real Holy Mountain, as the Bible knows it, is the uplifted consciousness which has dominion over all things; never a mountain in the outer world.

Emmet Fox

ONE SOLITARY LIFE

How do you explain the greatness of the Man whose birthday we celebrate on Christmas?

He was born in an obscure village, the child of a peasant woman. He grew up in another village. He worked in a carpenter shop until He was thirty, and then for three years was an itinerant preacher. He never wrote a book. He never held office. He never owned a home. He never traveled 200 miles from the place where He was born. He never did one of the things that usually accompany greatness. He had no credentials but Himself.

Although He walked the land over, curing the sick, giving sight to the blind, healing the lame, and raising people from the dead, the top established religious leaders turned against Him. His friends ran away. He was turned over to enemies. He went through the mockery of a trial. He was spat upon, flogged, and ridiculed. He was nailed to a cross between two thieves. While He was dying, the executioners gambled for the only piece of property He had on earth, and that was His robe. When He was dead, He was laid in a borrowed grave through the pity of a friend.

Nineteen wide centuries have come and gone, and today He is the central Figure of the human race and the Leader of the column of progress.

All the armies that ever marched, and all the navies that were ever built, and all the parliaments that ever sat, and all the kings that ever reigned, put together, have not affected the life of man upon this earth as has that One Solitary Life.

Author unknown

INVICTUS

Out of the night that covers me,
　　Black as the Pit from pole to pole,
I thank whatever gods may be
　　For my unconquerable soul.

In the fell clutch of circumstance
　　I have not winced nor cried aloud.
Under the bludgeonings of chance
　　My head is bloody, but unbowed.

Beyond this place of wrath and tears
　　Looms but the Horror of the shade,
And yet the menace of the years
　　Finds, and shall find, me unafraid.

It matters not now straight the gate,
　　How charged with punishments the scroll,
I am the master of my fate;
　　I am the captain of my soul.

William Ernest Henley

When I was a midshipman in officer training school, I had a brilliant and interesting commanding officer. All of us felt he deserved to be an admiral in charge of a fleet.

Captain Brown lectured us again and again on the importance of being able to give an order. He pointed out that orders were based on decisions. Some required time, and sometimes there *was* plenty of time for research, choice and planning. But there were "command decisions" which, in the heat of sea battles, had to be translated into orders instantaneously.

He repeatedly impressed us with the fact that as line officers we had to make decisions *our very own* and accept responsbility for their outcome. Furthermore, a man who could not give an order, who would not accept responsibility, who would not risk a mistake for whatever reason—whether perfectionism, poor self-esteem, or vanity—must not be in any command position. He pointed out that at sea, apathy, indecision, inhibition and paralysis could result not in mere mistakes but in catastrophic tragedies.

"Decide and order," he told us. To practice, each of us "gave orders" to marching platoons, sailboat crews, docking crews, shore battery drill crews. Our mistakes became fewer. Decisions and orders became easier. We also made mistakes and corrected them, increasing our flexibility, our morale and our fund of knowledge.

Real decisions do that: They integrate and unify various aspects of ourselves, translating theory into action. They increase self-esteem. Decision power increases geometrically, because the very act of decision-making breaks through inhibition and paralysis.

Conversely, prolonged apathy, indecision, paralysis and inhibition can result not just in mistakes but in disaster.

Theodore Isaac Rubin

WHAT IS RIGHT LIVING?

What is right living? Just to do your best
When worst seems easier. To bear the ills
Of daily life with patient cheerfulness
Nor waste dear time recounting them.
                                    To talk
Of hopeful things when doubt is in the air.
To count your blessings often, giving thanks,
And to accept your sorrows silently,
Nor question why you suffer. To accept
The whole of life as one perfected plan,
And welcome each event as part of it.
To work, and love your work; to trust, to pray
For larger usefulness and clearer sight.
This is right living, pleasing on God's eyes. . . .

Ella Wheeler Wilcox

THE SCOUT LAW

A Scout is:

TRUSTWORTHY.   A Scout tells the truth. He keeps his promises. Honesty is part of his code of conduct. People can depend on him.

LOYAL.   A Scout is true to his family, Scout leaders, friends, school and nation.

HELPFUL.

A Scout is concerned about other people. He does things willingly for others without pay or reward.

FRIENDLY.

A Scout is a friend to all. He is a brother to other Scouts. He seeks to understand others. He respects those with ideas and customs other than his own.

COURTEOUS.

A Scout is polite to everyone regardless of age or position. He knows good manners make it easier for people to get along together.

KIND.

A Scout understands there is strength in being gentle. He treats others as he wants to be treated. He does not hurt or kill harmless things without reason.

OBEDIENT.

A Scout follows the rules of his family, school, and troop. He obeys the laws of his community and country. If he thinks these rules and laws are unfair, he tries to have them changed in an orderly manner rather than disobey them.

CHEERFUL.

A Scout looks for the bright side of things. He cheerfully does tasks that come his way. He tries to make others happy.

THRIFTY.   A Scout works to pay his way to
                 help others. He saves for unfore-
                 seen needs. He protects and
                 conserves natural resources. He
                 carefully uses time and property.

BRAVE.   A Scout can face danger even if he
                 is afraid. He has the courage to
                 stand for what he thinks is right
                 even if others laugh at or threaten
                 him.

CLEAN.   A Scout keeps his body and mind
                 fit and clean. He goes around with
                 those who believe in living by these
                 same ideals. He helps keep his
                 home and community clean.

REVERENT.   A Scout is reverent toward God.
                 He is faithful in his religious duties.
                 He respects the beliefs of others.

Boy Scouts of America

ENTHUSIASM

THE DAWN

One morn I rose and looked upon the world.
"Have I been blind until this hour?" I said.
On every trembling leaf the sun had spread,
And was like golden tapestry unfurled;
And as the moments passed more light was hurled
Upon the drinking earth athirst for light;
And I, beholding all this wondrous sight,
Cried out aloud, "O God, I love Thy world!"
And since that waking, often I drink deep
The joy of dawn, and peace abides with me;
And though I know that I again shall see
Dark fear with withered hand approach my sleep,
More sure am I when lonely night shall flee,
At dawn the sun will bring good cheer to me.

Author unknown

When you have chosen a great purpose, and are certain
you have chosen well and wisely, concentrate upon it.
Bend your best energies to it. Guard yourself against
subtle and innumerable influences that tend to divert you

from it. Make that single great purpose *the definite aim of your daily life*. Be enthusiastic about it. Your thought and time will be solicited by many influences, and you will do well to take special means to protect yourself against them. Make your resolutions so clear and firm that nothing can lure you from your chosen path of purpose and duty. Substitute doing for dreaming, and achievement for wishing. The great things of the world are done by men who *specialize and concentrate*.

Grenville Kleiser

"I CAN"—THE TWO MOST POWERFUL WORDS IN YOUR VOCABULARY

"I can," said Cyrus W. Field, when the project of laying the first Atlantic cable was called a wild fantastic undertaking.

"I can," said Tracy Barnes when wiser people knew you couldn't make a transcontinental balloon flight across the U.S. After three thousand miles and five months in the air, he did it—all the way from San Diego, California, to Villas, New Jersey. Floating on capricious and unpredictable air movements, he had met exciting and dangerous experiences. He crashed into a mountain peak one hundred miles east of San Diego and spent three days in a hospital with a sprained back. He got lost in the Rockies and was separated from his ground crew for three days. Several times the balloon snagged on trees forcing delays. He landed near Pittsburgh.

It wasn't all rough going for the twenty-seven-year-old balloonist. He purposely drifted to the bottom of the Grand Canyon, parked his wicker basket and balloon, and went swimming in the Colorado River. From Nebraska to Pittsburgh it was a breeze. "Just great," Barnes said. The trip took about twice as long as estimated because of the unfavorable winds and the many mishaps.

"I can," said Birt Duncan. As a cast-off Negro child in the South, he was bumped from foster home to foster home. He remembers living with more than thirteen families from Arkansas to Mississippi. Often he'd fall asleep in classrooms because of improper nourishment. However, he now has a Ph.D. from Princeton in psychology and is completing work for an M.D. degree at the University of California in San Diego.

"What's really important is not what color your skin is—white or black," Birt Duncan says, "more important is — what color is your thinking? Red? Or Green? Think Green. Think Go! You cannot control the color of your skin, but you can determine the color of your thinking!"

"I can," said Romana Bañuelos. She was only sixteen years old when she married in Mexico. Two years and two sons later, she was divorced and working for one dollar a day in an El Paso laundry.

She heard she could do better in California, so with seven dollars in her pocket she took a bus to Los Angeles.

Starting by washing dishes and then taking whatever job she could get, she saved as much money as she could. When she had four hundred dollars, she and an aunt bought a little tortilla factory that had one tortilla machine and a grinder in a showcase in the front. When the aunt wanted to leave the business, Romana bought her share.

Romana's Mexican Food Products became the largest Mexican wholesale food concern in the nation, grossing five million dollars a year and Romana employs over three hundred people.

Romana was determined to lift the level of Mexican-Americans. "We need our own bank," she thought. She helped found the Pan American National Bank in East Los Angeles to serve the Mexican-American community. The bank's resources are more than twenty-two million dollars with 86 percent of the depository of Latin ancestry.

"I can," Romana said when Negative Thinking Experts told her "Mexican-Americans can't start a bank," "You're not qualified," "You can't make it." Undaunted, she spearheaded a committee which hired three attorneys who obtained a charter for the new bank.

"We opened the bank in a little trailer," she says, "but selling stock to the community was a problem. The people didn't have any faith in themselves. I used to go and ask them if they would buy stock and they said, 'Oh, Mrs. Bañuelos, what makes you think we can have a bank? We've tried for ten or fifteen years and always failed. You see, Mexican people are not bankers.'" The bank is now one of East Los Angeles' dynamic success stories.

"What's the major problem that keeps the Mexican-Americans down today?" she was asked. Her answer: "They believe the lie they have been told about themselves—that Mexicans are inferior! I was raised as a child in Mexico and no one can make me believe that lie! I'm proud of my Mexican ancestry!"

Today Romana Bañuelos has reached new heights of success. She was handpicked by the President of the United States to be the thirty-fourth treasurer of the United States!

Robert H. Schuller

Good attracts good. The man of upright character radiates an influence for good wherever he goes. Goodness of mind reflects itself in the face and manner so that it can be clearly read by other men. A genuinely good man is a constant guide and inspiration to those about him. It is amazing what the personal example of a good man will do in imparting *confidence, vitality, and enthusiasm* to his friends and associates. A virtuous life is often more persuasively eloquent than much verbal counsel. It is well to mingle freely with good men, that their influence and example may be felt and utilized, but it is still better to be a good man. Goodness has a power all its own to *instruct, persuade, and inspire.*

Grenville Kleiser

PROGRESS

_____

A PSALM OF LIFE

Tell me not, in mournful numbers,
　"Life is but an empty dream!"
For the soul is dead that slumbers
　And things are not what they seem.

Life is real! Life is earnest;
　And the grave is not its goal;
"Dust thou art, to dust returnest,"
　Was not spoken of the soul.

Not enjoyment, and not sorrow,
　Is our destined end or way;
But to act, that each to-morrow
　Find us farther than to-day.

Art is long, and Time is fleeting,
　And our hearts, though stout and brave.
Still, like muffled drums, are beating
　Funeral marches to the grave.

In the world's broad field of battle,
  In the bivouac of Life,
Be not like dumb, driven cattle!
  Be a hero in the strife!

Trust no Future, howe'er pleasant!
  Let the dead past bury its dead!
Act,—act in the living Present!
  Heart within and God o'erhead!

Lives of great men all remind us
  We can make our lives sublime,
And, departing, leave behind us
  Footprints on the sands of Time;

Footprints, that perhaps another,
  Ailing o'er life's solemn main,
A forlorn and shipwrecked brother,
  Seeing, shall take heart again.

Let us, then, be up and doing,
  With a heart for any fate;
Still achieving, still pursuing,
  Learn to labour and to wait.

Henry Wadsworth Longfellow

TEN COMMANDMENTS FOR
POSSIBILITY THINKERS

There are ten rules you must follow as you read these pages. Ignore them and you will deprive yourself of immeasurable excitement, achievement, and success. I call these principles the ten commandments for possibility thinkers. It is imperative that you acquaint yourself with them now—at the outset—before you ever try to expand your thinking.

1. You will never vote no to any idea because "It's impossible."
2. You will never block a helpful thought because it entails problems, or wait to begin until you find a solution to every problem.
3. You will never oppose a possibility because you've never done it and can't imagine how it could be done.
4. You will never obstruct a plan because it runs a risk of failure.
5. You will never cooperate in defeating a potentially good suggestion because you can see something wrong with it.
6. You will never squelch a creative idea because no one else has ever succeeded in perfecting it.
7. You will never declare any constructive concept to be impossible because you lack the time, money, brains, energy, talent, or skill to exploit it.

8. You will never discard a plan or a project just because it's imperfect.

9. You will never resist a proposal because you didn't think of it, you won't get the credit, you won't personally benefit from it, or you may not live to see and enjoy it.

10. You will never quit because you've reached the end of the rope. Tie a knot and hang on.

Now, start dreaming! Be sure to make your dreams big enough for God to fit in!

Robert H. Schuller

To laugh often and much;
   to win the respect of
intelligent people and the
   affection of children;
to earn the appreciation of honest
   critics and endure the betrayal of false friends;
   to appreciate beauty;

to find the best in others; to leave
   the world a bit better, whether by
a healthy child, a garden patch or
   a redeemed social condition;

to know even one life
has breathed easier because
you lived.

This is to have succeeded.

Ralph Waldo Emerson

The immediate future of our race is indescribably
hopeful. . . . In contact with the flux of cosmic consciousness all religions known and named today will be
melted down. The human soul will be revolutionized.
Religion will absolutely dominate the race. . . . The
evidence of immortality will live in every heart as sight in
every eye. Doubt of God and of eternal life will be as
impossible as is now doubt of existence; the evidence of
each will be the same. . . . Each soul will feel and know
itself to be immortal, will feel and know that the entire
universe with all its good and with all its beauty is for it
and belongs to it forever.

Richard Maurice Bucke

Many competent people feel great frustration because
of rules and bureaucratic restrictions. Frustration can
frequently be replaced with satisfaction when the competent employee is granted the authority to utilize his power
to do his job or manage his department in his own way.

In this manner attention is focused on realistic objectives rather than upon ritualistic procedures. Improved effectiveness follows when administrators show respect for competent people and translate that respect into patterns of freedom to use individual initiative. This satisfies the need for self-fulfillment and for feeling esteemed and valued.

Laurence J. Peter

Down deep in every human soul is a hidden longing, impulse, and ambition to do something fine and enduring. This secret intimation from within is in truth a summons to rise above the dead level of mediocrity and to use your powers to large purpose. As you listen to this inner voice and heed its divine command, you will not be content with a life of commonplace endeavor, but will set your eyes upon *some great and lofty purpose*. There will come to you a new and wonderful revelation of the exalted powers placed in your keeping, and a deeper realization of *your personal responsibility to God*. He has endowed you with supreme gifts as well as with the faculties to use them aright. If you are willing, great things are possible to you.

Grenville Kleiser

CHRISTMAS—ITS
SCIENTIFIC MEANING

Modern scientific research has revealed that the primal
vehicles of life—atoms, cells, and so forth—are composed
of principles that bring them under a spiritual rather than
a material classification, and that they are linked with a
field of causation in which all things are possible. Instead
of the atom being the material ultimate of creation, its
processes have blossomed into a realm where it assumes
the role of deity and its creative possibilities are described
by scientists with a splendor and assurance of accomplishment that makes all the unbelievable tales of magic and
the heavenly dreams of saints seem tawdry and cheap.

A very large number of persons who believe that
religion is more than emotion and soul ecstasy welcome
joyfully these announcements of the scientists that they
have discovered a kingdom quite superior to the physical,
yet related to it by laws that can be applied by those who
understand them.

That the potential assets of these invisible elements are
far beyond anything we have ever conceived in our
wildest dreams is asserted by these modern scientific seers
and prophets. If what they have described as existing in
this newly discovered fourth dimension were printed in
the Bible, it would not be believed. The story of Joshua's
stopping the sun for a whole day and of Jonah's living
three days in the whale's belly are not to be compared in

credibility with the claim of Sir Oliver Lodge that there is power enough in a cubic inch of ether to run a forty-horsepower engine forty million years! This claim of Sir Oliver Lodge is tame compared with numerous others voiced in the books of these scientists.

Jesus described this kingdom of the heavens, or fourth dimension, in many parables and comparisons. That it was of more value than all earthly things He illustrated in the parable of the man who discovered a treasure hidden in a field and sold all he had and bought that field. Science is bringing certain greatly treasured elements of that fourth-dimension kingdom into the earth, and we are enjoying their coming in light, heat, power, radio, and ultraviolet rays quickening growth in vegetables and fruits, and above all vitalizing the bodies of men, women, and children.

This is but the beginning of the prophecy written in Revelation 21:10–11, 24, RSV: "And in the Spirit he carried me away to a great, high mountain, and showed me the holy city Jerusalem coming down out of heaven from God, having the glory of God. . . . By its light shall the nations walk; and the kings of the earth shall bring their glory into it."

This does not say that Jerusalem, a type of heaven, is far away in the heavens and that we are going to it through death, but it states that heaven is to be set up in the earth and the "kings of the earth" (the spiritually developed) are to enter into it and bring their "glory" into it. Physical science is making visible in mechanical appliances only a few of these marvelous forces from the heavens, but even now the great need is spiritually

developed persons who can lay hold of the supermind
elements and restore the physical organism of the race to
its original vitality, even eternal life. Scientists tell us that
they are developing powers beyond our ability to control
them. Scientists do not claim that the fourth dimension,
with its amazing energies, is identical with the kingdom
of the heavens that Jesus described in parables, but some
of them have stated that they are satisfied that Jesus was
familiar with the ether and used its superpower in His
miracles. However, as they become more familiar with the
evidences of a directive mind in the design and activity of
these invisible forces, they will be compelled to admit that
there is something more than blind matter behind the
universe.

Sir James Jeans, the eminent British scientist, in his
book *The Mysterious Universe*, says:

> *Although we are still far from any positive knowledge, it
> seems possible that there may be some factor, for which we
> have so far found no better name than fate, operating in
> nature to neutralize the cast-iron inevitability of the old
> law of causation. The future may not be as unalterably
> determined by the past as we used to think; in part at least
> it may rest on the knees of whatever gods there may be.*

In a public address Professor Jeans stated flatly that
science no longer holds that we live in a world of solid
matter, but that on the contrary *we are beginning to suspect
that we live in a universe of waves, and nothing but waves.*
He refers, of course, to the etheric waves that penetrate
all space and all matter.

The theory of Dalton that the atom is the foundation
and ultimate of all matter has been definitely exploded, as
stated by our American scientist, Professor Millikan:

> *Matter is no longer a mere game of marbles played by blind
> men. An atom is now an amazingly complicated organism,
> possessing many interrelated bodies and exhibiting many
> functions and properties—energy, radiation, waves and so
> forth, quite as mysterious as any that used to masquerade
> under the name of "mind." Hence the phrases "All is
> matter" and "All is mind" have now become mere
> shibboleths devoid of meaning.*

Metaphysicians protest that the phrase "All is mind"
has not lost its meaning, but has arisen to first place as a
concise statement of the underlying cause of all existence.

Right here is where scientists need to realize that they
are still blind men playing a game of marbles, as
compared with what they will be when they awaken their
latent spiritual faculties and behold the majesty, harmony,
and power of the unseen fourth dimension, which they
now postulate as existing but which they have never
seen. . . .

In His personality as Jesus, He was a man among men;
but the God-Mind in Him, called Christ, had been
advanced far beyond the consciousness of anyone in our
race. But as He stated, we can through Him come into
the same sphere of glory—that is, of spiritual power—
that He occupied. *But as many as received him, to them
gave he power to become the sons of God, even to them that
believe on his name* (Jn. 1:12, KJV).

This understanding of the scientific and orderly
construction of our eternal body should appeal to all

logical minds and give them a firm foundation for the hope of eternal life. God does not at death give us a heavenly body, but makes it possible for us to earn that body by honest work, and thus escape death. Jesus "advanced in wisdom and stature." So we may also grow, if we seek to know and conform to the divine law. Thousands of persons are in the new birth and do not realize it. When the angel told Mary that she had conceived by the Holy Spirit she questioned it.

Those who have been faithful in following Jesus throughout the centuries will finally form a world federation in His name, which will be the nucleus of a new race, through whom the kingdom of the heavens will be developed in this earth, and it will be ruled by the "kings of the earth."

With the understanding that the birth of Jesus represents the beginning of a process by which all of us may transform our mortal body into a spiritual body, we see the scientific meaning of Paul's statement that *This corruptible must put on incorruption, and this mortal must put on immortality* (1 Cor. 15:53, KJV). Paul thought that this transformation was to be accomplished "in the twinkling of an eye," by a miracle, but now that we have science showing us that all things are under law and that the cells of our bodies are inherently immortal, we see that what we looked forward to as a miracle to take place after death can be brought to pass right here and now. The new Christ body is not formed in the dead but in the living. *He is not God of the Dead, but of the living* (Mt. 22:32, RSV).

Charles Fillmore

'Tis the good reader that makes the good book; in every book he finds passages which seem confidences or asides hidden from all else and unmistakably meant for his ear; the profit of books is according to the sensibility of the reader; the profoundest thought or passion sleeps as in a mine, until it is discovered by an equal mind and heart.

Ralph Waldo Emerson

Youth is not a time of life, it's a state of mind: it is a temper of the will, a quality of the imagination, a vigor of the emotions, a predominance of courage over timidity, of the appetite for adventure over love of ease. Nobody grows old by merely living a number of years; people grow old only by deserting their ideals. Years wrinkle the skin, but to give up enthusiasm wrinkles the soul. Worry, doubt, self-distrust, fear and despair—these are the long, long years that bow the head and turn the growing spirit back to dust. Whether seventy or sixteen, there is in every being's heart the love of wonder, the sweet amazement at the stars and the star-like things and thought, the undaunted challenge of events, the unfailing childlike appetite for what-next, and the joy and the game of life.

You are as young as your faith, as old as your doubt, as young as your self-confidence, as old as your fear, as young as your hope, as old as your despair. So long as your heart receives messages of beauty, cheer, courage, grandeur and power from the earth, from man and from the infinite, so long are you young. When the wires are all down and all the central place of your heart is covered with the snows of pessimism and the ice of cynicism, then you are grown old indeed and may God have mercy on your soul.

Author unknown

WINNING THROUGH HUMILITY

VI

I N my book *The Humble Approach*, I wrote: "By learning humility, we find that the purpose of life on earth is vastly deeper than any human mind can grasp. Diligently, each child of God should seek to find and obey God's purpose, but none be so egotistical as to think that he or she comprehends the infinite mind of God."

The problem with pride is that it puts you in competition with everyone and everything and thus makes it difficult to seek the truth. As C. S. Lewis says, "Pride gets no pleasure out of having something, only out of having more of it than the next man."

Humility and pride—the former is in tune with God, whereas the latter is out of harmony with His teachings. Pride can learn this lesson of great value from humility—that one need have no enemies or rivals, that in the eyes of God no one is better or worse than anyone else.

HUMILITY

A PRAYER

The supreme prayer of my heart is not to be learned,
rich, famous, powerful, or "good," but simply to be
radiant. I desire to radiate health, cheerfulness, calm
courage and good will. I wish to live without hate, whim,
jealousy, envy, fear. I wish to be simple, honest, frank,
natural, clean in mind and clean in body, unaffected—
ready to say "I do not know," if it be so, and to meet all
men on an absolute equality—to face any obstacle and
meet every difficulty unabashed and unafraid.

I wish others to live their lives, too—up to their
highest, fullest and best. To that end I pray that I may
never meddle, interfere, dictate, give advice that is not
wanted, or assist when my services are not needed. If I
can help people, I'll do it by giving them a chance to help
themselves; and if I can uplift or inspire, let it be by
example, inference, and suggestion, rather than by
injunction and dictation. That is to say, I desire to be
radiant—to radiate life.

Elbert Hubbard

When man becomes humble in his approach to God, then he can think and speak in this way:

Billions of stars in the Milky Way are upheld in the dynamic embrace of God's being, and He is much more.

Billions and billions of stars in other galaxies are creatively sustained in God in the same way, and He is much more.

Time and space and energy are all included within the power of God's presence, and He is much more.

Men who dwell in three dimensions can apprehend only a very little of God's multitude of dimensions.

God infinitely surpasses all the things seen and also the vastly greater abundance of things unseen by man.

God is the only ultimate reality—all else is fleeting and contingent.

The awesome mysteries of magnetism, gratitude, joy, and love are all from God himself, and He is much more.

Five billion people live on earth and live and move and have their being in God, and He is much more.

Untold billions of beings on planets of millions of other galaxies are what they are in God, and He is much more.

God is beginning to create His universe and allows each of us His children to participate in small ways in this creative evolution.

God is infinitely great and also infinitely small. He is present in each of our inmost thoughts, each of our trillions of body cells, and each of the wave patterns in each cell.

God embraces all of us within the presence and power of His being, but we are a very little of all that subsists in Him.

John Marks Templeton

ANSWERED PRAYER

I asked God for strength,
   the I might achieve,
 I was made weak,
   that I might learn humbly to obey . . .
I asked for health,
   that I might do greater things,
 I was given infirmity,
   that I might do better things . . .
I asked for riches,
   that I might be happy,
 I was given poverty,
   that I might be wise . . .
I asked for power,
   that I might have the praise of men,
 I was given weakness,
   that I might feel the need of God . . .
I asked for all things,
   that I might enjoy life,
 I was given life,
   that I might enjoy all things . . .

I got nothing that I asked for—
but everything I had hoped for
Almost despite myself,
my unspoken prayers were answered.
I am among all men most richly blessed.

Unknown Confederate soldier

DESIDERATA

Go placidly amid the noise & haste, & remember what peace there may be in silence. As far as possible without surrender be on good terms with all persons. Speak your truth quietly & clearly; and listen to others, even the dull & ignorant; they too have their story.

Avoid loud & aggressive persons, they are vexations to the spirit. If you compare yourself with others, you may become vain & bitter; for always there will be greater & lesser persons than yourself. Enjoy your achievements as well as your plans.

Keep interested in your own career, however humble; it is a real possession in the changing fortunes of time. Exercise caution in your business affairs; for the world is full of trickery. But let this not blind you to what virtue there is; many persons strive for high ideals; and everywhere life is full of heroism.

206

Be yourself. Especially, do not feign affection. Neither be cynical about love; for in the face of all aridity & disenchantment it is perennial as the grass.

Take kindly the counsel of the years, gracefully surrendering the things of youth. Nurture strength of spirit to shield you in sudden misfortune. But do not distress yourself with imaginings. Many fears are born of fatigue & loneliness. Beyond a wholesome discipline, be gentle with yourself.

You are a child of the universe, no less than the trees & the stars; you have a right to be here. And whether or not it is clear to you, no doubt the universe is unfolding as it should.

Therefore be at peace with God, whatever you conceive Him to be, and whatever your labors & aspirations, in the noisy confusion of life keep peace with your soul.

With all its sham, drudgery & broken dreams, it is still a beautiful world. Be careful. Strive to be happy.

Author unknown

It's hard to be an agnostic up here in the *Spirit of St. Louis,* aware of the frailty of man's devices, a part of the universe between its earth and stars. If one dies, all this goes on existing in a plan so perfectly balanced, so wonderfully simple, so incredibly complex that it's far beyond our comprehension—worlds and moon revolving; planets orbiting around suns; suns flung with apparent recklessness through space. There's the infinite magnitude of the universe; there's the infinite detail to its matter— the outer star, the inner atom. And man conscious of it all—a worldly audience to what if not to God?

Charles Lindbergh

In my dealing with my child, my Latin and Greek, my accomplishments and my money stead me nothing; but as much soul as I have avails. If I am willful, he sets his will against mine, one for one, and leaves me, if I please, the degradation of beating him by my superiority of strength. But if I renounce my will and act for the soul, setting that up as umpire between us two, out of his young eyes looks the same soul; he reveres and loves with me.

The soul is the perceiver and revealer of truth. We know truth when we see it, let sceptic and scoffer say what they choose. Foolish people ask you, when you have spoken what they do not wish to hear, "How do you know it is truth, and not an error of your own?" We know truth when we see it, from opinion, as we know when we are awake that we are awake. It was a grand sentence of Emanuel Swedenborg, which would alone indicate the greatness of that man's perception,—"It is no proof of a man's understanding to be able to affirm whatever he pleases; but to be able to discern that what is true is true, and that what is false is false,—this is the mark and character of intelligence."

Ralph Waldo Emerson

We are perched on the frontiers of future knowledge. Even though we stand upon the enormous mountain of information collected over the last five centuries of scientific progress, we have only fleeting glimpses of the future. To a large extent, the future lies before us like a vast wilderness of unexplored reality. The God who created and sustains His evolving universe through eons of progress and development has not placed our generation at the tag end of the creative process. He has placed us at a new beginning. We are here for the future.

Our role is crucial. As human beings we are endowed with mind and spirit. We can think, imagine, and dream. We can search for future trends through the rich diversity of human thought. God permits us in some ways to be co-creators with Him in His continuing act of creation.

Scientists have steadily been changing their concepts of the universe and laws of nature, but the progression is always away from smaller self-centered or human-centered concepts. Evidence is always accumulating that things seen are only one aspect of the vastly greater unseen realities. Human observational abilities are very limited and so are our mental abilities. Should we not focus

ourselves on the unseen realities and not on the fleeting
appearances? Should we not kneel down in humility
and worship the awesome, infinite, omniscient, eternal
Creator?

By learning humility, we find that the purpose of life
on earth is vastly deeper than any human mind can
grasp. Diligently, each child of God should seek to find
and obey God's purpose, but none be so egotistical as
to think that he or she comprehends the infinite mind
of God.

Every person's concept of God is too small. Through
humility we can begin to get into true perspective the
infinity of God. This is the humble approach. Are we
ready to begin the formulation of a humble theology
which can never become obsolete? This would be a
theology really centered on God and not our own little
selves.

John Marks Templeton

Love and serve humanity.

Be original. Be inventive. Do not imitate. Be yourself.
Know yourself.

Stand on your own ground. Do not lean on the
borrowed staff of others.

Think your own thoughts.

There is no saint without a past. There is no sinner
without a future.

Let your life be like unto a rose; though silent it speaks a language of fragrance.

Be deaf and dumb concerning the faults of others.

Do not listen to gossip. Silence the tale-bearer with virtuous conversation.

Never argue with anyone concerning his religious beliefs. Religion is Love and Fellowship and not theological dogmas and creeds.

Mirza Ahmad Sohrab

If the earth is a school, who are the teachers? One teacher is called adversity. Why did God put souls into a world of tribulations? Why did He not just make souls perfect in the first place? Is not God vastly more far-sighted and infinitely wise than we are? Maybe from God's perspective the sorrows and tribulations of this earth are the best way to educate souls.

Growth can come through trial and self-discipline. There is a wealth of evidence indicating that too much prosperity without work weakens character and causes us to become self-centered rather than God-centered. Spiritual growth and happiness do not come from getting but from learning to give. The great souls are the most rapidly growing souls. Trees and human bodies are limited in growth both in space and time, but is there any evidence that the individual soul is limited in its growth?

How could a soul understand divine joy or be thankful for heaven if it had not previously experienced earth?

How could a soul comprehend the joy of surrender to God's will if it had never witnessed the hell people make on earth by trying to rely on self-will or on another frail human or on a soul-less, human-made government?

Maybe the earth was designed as a place of hardship because it is the best way to build a soul—the best way to teach spiritual joy versus the bodily ills. Why was it said that into every life some rain must fall? It is apparent that sometimes a great soul does not develop until that person has gone through some great tragedy. Let us humbly admit that God knows best how to build a soul. If the soul were born perfect, how would it understand or appreciate the absence of pain and sorrow? As a good father does not do his son's homework for him, so our Heavenly Father does what helps us to grow, not what we ask for.

John Marks Templeton

To be honest, to be kind, to earn a little and spend a little less; to make, upon the whole, a family happier by his presence, to renounce when that shall be necessary, and not be embittered; to keep a few friends, but these without capitulation—above all, on the same grim condition to keep friends with himself—here is a task for all that a man has of fortitude and delicacy.

Robert Louis Stevenson

PRIDE

According to Christian teachers, the essential vice, the utmost of evil, is Pride. Unchastity, anger, greed, drunkenness, and all that, are mere flea-bites in comparison: it was through Pride that the devil became the devil: Pride leads to every other vice: it is the complete anti-God state of mind.

Does this seem exaggerated? If you want to find out how proud you are, the easiest way is to ask yourself, "How much do I dislike it when other people snub me, or patronize me, or show off?" The point is that each person's pride is in competition with everyone else's pride. It is because I wanted to be the big noise at the party that I am so annoyed at someone else being the big noise. Two of a trade never agree. Now what you want to get clear is that Pride is *essentially* competitive—is competitive by its very nature—while the other vices are competitive only, so to speak, by accident. Pride gets no pleasure out of having something, only out of having more of it than the next man. We say that people are proud of being rich, or clever, or good-looking, but they are not. They are proud of being richer, or cleverer, or better-looking than others. If everyone else became equally rich, or clever, or good-looking, there would be nothing to be proud about. It is the comparison that

213

makes you proud: the pleasure of being above the rest.
Once the element of competition has gone, pride has
gone. That is why I say that Pride is essentially competitive in a way the other vices are not. The sexual
impulse may drive two men into competition if they both
want the same girl. But that is only by accident; they
might just as likely have wanted two different girls. But a
proud man will take your girl from you, not because he
wants her, but just to prove to himself that he is a better
man than you. Greed may drive men into competition if
there is not enough to go 'round; but the proud man,
even when he has got more than he can possibly want,
will try to get still more just to assert his power. Nearly
all those evils in the world which people put down to
greed or selfishness are really far more the result of Pride.

Take it with money. Greed will certainly make a man
want money, for the sake of a better house, better
holidays, better things to eat and drink. But only up to a
point. What is it that makes a man with £10,000 a year
anxious to get £20,000 a year? It is not the greed for
more pleasure. £10,000 will give all the luxuries that any
man can really enjoy. It is Pride—the wish to be richer
than some other rich man, and (still more) the wish for
power. For, of course, power is what Pride really enjoys:
there is nothing makes a man feel so superior to others as
being able to move them about like toy soldiers. What
makes a pretty girl spread misery wherever she goes by
collecting admirerers? Certainly not her sexual instinct:
that kind of girl is quite often sexually frigid. It is Pride.
What is it that makes a political leader or a whole nation
go on and on, demanding more and more? Pride again.
Pride is competitive by its very nature: that is why it goes

on and on. If I am a proud man, then, as long as there is one man in the whole world more powerful, or richer, or cleverer than I, he is my rival and my enemy.

The Christians are right: it is Pride which has been the chief cause of misery in every nation and every family since the world began. Other vices may sometimes bring people together: you may find good fellowship and jokes and friendliness among drunken people or unchaste people. But Pride always means enmity—it *is* enmity. And not only enmity between man and man but enmity to God.

In God you come up against something which is in every respect immeasurably superior to yourself. Unless you know God as that—and, therefore, know yourself as nothing in comparison—you do not know God at all. As long as you are proud, you cannot know God. A proud man is always looking down on things and people: and, of course, as long as you are looking down, you cannot see something that is above you.

That raises a terrible question. How is it that people who are quite obviously eaten up with Pride can say they believe in God and appear to themselves very religious? I am afraid it means they are worshiping an imaginary God. They theoretically admit themselves to be nothing in the presence of this phantom God, but are really all the time imagining how He approves of them and thinks them far better than ordinary people: that is, they pay a pennyworth of imaginary humility to Him and get out of it a pound's worth of Pride toward their fellowmen. I suppose it was of those people Christ was thinking when He said that some would preach about Him and cast out devils in His name, only to be told at the end of the world that He had never known them. And any of us may at any moment be in this deathtrap. Luckily, we have a test. Whenever we find that our religious life is making us feel that we are good—above all, that we are better than someone else—I think we may be sure that we are being acted on, not by God, but by the devil. The real test of being in the presence of God is that you either forget about yourself altogether or see yourself as a small, dirty object. It is better to forget about yourself altogether.

It is a terrible thing that the worst of all the vices can smuggle itself into the very center of our religious life. But you can see why. The other, and less bad, vices come from the devil working on us through our animal nature. But this does not come through our animal nature at all. It comes direct from Hell. It is purely spiritual: consequently it is far more subtle and deadly. For the same reason, Pride can often be used to beat down the simpler vices. Teachers, in fact, often appeal to a boy's Pride, or, as they call it, his self-respect, to make him behave decently: many a man has overcome cowardice, or lust, or ill temper by learning to think that they are beneath his dignity—that is, by Pride. The devil laughs. He is perfectly content to see you becoming chaste and brave and self-controlled provided, all the time, he is setting up in you the Dictatorship of Pride—just as he would be quite content to see your chilblains cured if he was allowed, in return, to give you cancer. For Pride is spiritual cancer: it eats up the very possibility of love, or contentment, or even common sense.

C. S. Lewis

BUILDING A
CATHEDRAL

VII

ONE of my all-time favorite stories, repeated a few pages on—and one that extols the virtues of creativity, perseverance, and work—was told by Edward Pulling, a great educator. During the Middle Ages, he tells us, a government inspector went to a building site in France to see how laborers felt about their work. The first man he approached complained about the heat, and the primitive tools he had to use, and expressed his boredom with the task at hand. The second man felt his work served a useful purpose and, at least, it was a job that helped him support his family. The third man, when questioned, raised his arms to the sky and said: "Why, can't you see? I'm building a cathedral!"

Creativity, perseverance, and work—by pursuing these three virtues, by seeing the results of our efforts as a kind of cathedral, we can fill our lives with meaning.

CREATIVITY

In the Old Testament, the book of Leviticus tells of a sacred custom called the "escaped goat." When the troubles of the people became too much, a healthy male goat was brought into the temple. In a solemn ceremony, the highest priest of the tribe placed his hands on the head of the goat and recited the list of woes. The problems were then transferred onto the goat and the goat was set free, taking the troubles away with him.

That was about four thousand years ago, but we still use "scape goats" today. We frequently use other people, other things in our lives to avoid accepting the responsibility of who we are and what we do. Instead of working on what is going on inside us, we try to blame that which is around us.

It's always easier and more convenient to assume the answer lies elsewhere or with others. When life gets tough at work, we start to think, "It's this job." We often use our job as a scapegoat for the wrong stuff circulating inside us. Attitude at work can be summarized by this wonderful story, told by Edward Pulling, a great educator.

Back in the Middle Ages, a dispatcher went out to determine how laborers felt about their work. He went to a building site in France.

He approached the first worker and asked, "What are you doing?"

"What are you, blind?" the worker snapped back. "I'm cutting these impossible boulders with primitive tools and putting them together the way the boss tells me. I'm sweating under this blazing sun, it's back-breaking work, and it's boring me to death!"

The dispatcher quickly backed off and retreated to a second worker. He asked the same question: "What are you doing?"

The worker replied, "I'm shaping these boulders into useable forms, which are then assembled according to the architect's plans. It's hard work and sometimes it gets repetitive, but I earn five francs a week and that supports the wife and kids. It's a job. Could be worse."

Somewhat encouraged, the dispatcher went on to a third worker. "And what are you doing?" he asked.

"Why, can't you see?" said the worker as he lifted his arms to the sky, "I'm building a cathedral!"

Now *that's* the joy of working.

Denis Waitley and Reni Witt

LIMBERING UP YOUR MIND

May I emphasize the thought that "contrary thinking" is one of the best ways to limber up your mind; and I hope you'll try it out. You've noticed how, at a school or college baseball game, the coach has the ball batted around the bases to limber up the infield, before the team gets down to the business of scoring hits, put-outs, and errors.

You can limber up your mind the same way—by tossing ideas back and forth. Countless creative ideas have been originated by one idea bringing to mind another. You can enhance the game by throwing in contrary ideas. There is nothing like disagreements to bring out a fresh thought.

Try batting the ball around the next time you have a problem to solve. Toss in all the contrary angles you think of. You will find this pro and con method most helpful in rounding out the information you require for a sound solution.

Humphrey B. Neill

The cause of a great many of the troubles people encounter rests in the fact that they seem to have developed a sort of lethargy, which demands that everything be brought to them on a silver platter without their having to do anything about it. This is a nice idea if it would work, but it doesn't, for it overlooks the fact that basic and fundamental to all existence is acativity and creativity. If this dictum is ignored living is deprived of all meaning.

Do you feel that the world owes you a living, that life should provide you with all your desires and needs without your doing anything about it? The truth of the matter is that all you could possibly need has already been provided for you! There is no reason for any person to sit back and complain that the world has done him wrong, has withheld the things that make living worthwhile. As long as you acknowledge that the Mind back of the universe is intelligent and within It rests the possibility of all good things, then you can realize that everything has already been given you, is ever accessible to you. The problem is to what degree and extent you are able to recognize and accept this.

Life owes you nothing but you are eternally in debt to Life. You are the one who is withholding yourself from Life. What do you owe, and to whom do you owe it? You are only able to receive to the extent to which you are able to give. To start with, you are alive, an expression of the One Life. To the extent you are able to embody and express what you feel must be Its fundamental nature, to that extent you are able to experience more of It. Life has been given to you, now it is up to you to do something with it. Life is good, creative, dynamic, purposeful and joyous, and you have to express these qualities. You have to let them flow through you into the world about you. If you have the idea that life has done you wrong, the only thing that really has happened is that you have done yourself wrong.

If you feel that life is a continual conflict, you unintentionally are isolating yourself from the Source which can fulfill your every need. The battle you must wage is not with the world, the argument you must win is not with God, but with yourself. In many respects, you are your own worst enemy. When your thoughts and acts are constructive, then you will find that you already have what you once thought was owed to you. Then all conflict and struggle is dissolved.

You can make a down payment on your debt and start to eliminate a feeling that Life owes you something by this simple procedure: stop feeling sorry for yourself and begin to use your God-given ability to think in a constructive manner. Start to live now, for Life can never be more to you than It is right now. It can never provide you with more than you can consciously accept. When you change your pattern of thinking, and concern yourself with what you can contribute to Life, you will be surprised at what you will start receiving.

Certain sayings have become so familiar that the truths they contain are overlooked. Such ideas as "The gift is most to the giver"; "Give, and it shall be given unto you"; and "As ye would that men should do to you, do ye also to them likewise," should be re-examined. The world can supply you with abundant living, but not on the basis that it is owed to you. You must become an active participant in life, contributing the most that you have in the best manner possible.

You are not dealing with pretty platitudes, nice ideas, or beautiful sayings. Instead you realize that you are living in a lawful universe and that, regardless of the experience about which you may be concerned, things happen only as a result of an adequate cause. You cannot receive without first giving, and what you receive is in direct proportion to the extent of the giving of your thought, time, and abilities. Proper creative thought, backed up with appropriate action, opens the doorway for the universe to reciprocate with abundance, "good measure, pressed down . . . and running over."

Willis Kinnear

An old man was planting a sapling on the front lawn of his house. A young fellow passed by, stopped, watched the old man dig and asked what he was doing. "Planting a peach tree," the old man replied. Puzzled by this, the young man said, "I don't mean to sound brash, but it takes many years for a small tree like the one you're planting to bear fruit. Do you really expect to eat the fruit from this tree?" Rather than be offended by the question, the old man answered, "Probably not, but I've been eating fruit all my life from trees other people planted. Maybe it's my turn to plant a tree."

Author unknown

PERSEVERANCE

One of the greatest demonstrations of how a motivated positive thinker reaches goals is the story of the unforgettable Olympic champion Jesse Owens. I had the privilege of personally knowing this superb athlete, this great American. Some sportswriters judged him to be one of the greatest athletes in the history of this country. Jesse Owens himself vigorously disclaimed such high evaluation, but there is no doubt about his athletic prowess or about his greatness as a sincere Christian and as a notable human being.

One evening during a dinner program of the Ohio Newspaper Publishers' Association in Columbus, Ohio, I sat by Jesse Owens at the head table. I got him to talk about his life and career, and he related the following story. He was born into a black family of extremely limited means. "We were poor materially but rich spiritually." He also said that as a young boy, he was of slight build, even skinny, with a below-average physique. But his believing, positive mother told him that he was destined to do great things in life, that he was going to be somebody. He didn't see how that was possible. His family was poor and had no influence. Everything seemed against him, but his mother kept reminding him of the

Lord by saying, "You just be a believer and keep faithful. You will be led."

One day at a school assembly the speaker was Charlie Paddock, one of the most famous athletes of the time. On many a sports page he was hailed as "the fastest human being alive." I saw him run once in the Boston Arena, and he was like greased lightning. Having long since retired from his athletic career, Paddock gave his time to motivating kids everywhere, and he had a tremendous influence on youths.

Over a thousand kids packed the school auditorium that day to hear the renowned runner speak, and little Jesse Owens was in the front row. Owens said that Charlie Paddock walked to the front of the stage, put both hands in his hip pockets, let a deep silence fall, and in a full strong voice shot out the question, "Do you know who you are? You don't, eh? Well, I'm here to tell you. You are Americans, and you are the children of God. You can be somebody. You can be anything you want to be if you have a goal and will work and believe and have good moral character. You really can be what you want to be with the help of the good God."

Jesse Owens told me that in that moment, in a flash, he knew just what he wanted to be; his goal was instantly formed. He wanted to be the next Charlie Paddock, the fastest human being alive. He could scarcely wait for the speech to end, and immediately he rushed up and clasped Paddock's hand. With a touch of awe in his voice, he told me, "When I grabbed Charlie's hand, an electric impulse passed up my arm and through my body."

Then he rushed to the coach, shouting, "Coach, I have a dream, I have a dream. I'm going to be the next Charlie Paddock. I'm going to be the fastest man on earth!" The coach was a wise man, a motivator and guide. He put his arm around the shoulders of the frail little boy. "That's right, Jesse. Have a dream, a big dream. You will never go any higher than you can dream. But you can go as high as you dream if you work at it, believe in it, and stick to it. To reach your dream, you must climb a ladder on which there are four rungs. Mark them well. They are (1) determination, (2) dedication, (3) discipline, and (4) attitude."

The coach went on to say that attitude is of primary importance, even more than the other three qualities taken together, because attitude deals with how a person thinks and believes. And before anyone can be dedicated, determined and disciplined, he must make a mental and spiritual commitment to the goal. He must continue to think positively about it all the way to its attainment.

I was fascinated as Jesse Owens told me this story of his awakening to his possibilities, his goal, his dream and how it could come true. What followed? He thrilled the world in the 1936 Olympic Games by winning four gold medals. He tied the record for the one-hundred-meter race and ran the two-hundred-meter race faster than it had ever been run before. His broad jump record set in the games lasted for twenty-two years, and his performance on the relay team was spectacular. And finally, when the American Hall of Athletic Fame was established, the name that led all the rest was that of the frail little boy from Cleveland who followed a dream, a goal to athletic immortality. Reflect on the story of Jesse Owens and know, really know in your heart, that you too as a positive thinker can reach your goal.

To help you do just that, here are ten "of course you can" principles. Engrave them on your mind. Believe they will work when used. By applying them, the positive thinker gets powerful results.

1. Stamp your goal indelibly on your mind.
2. Always imagine yourself as succeeding with God's help.
3. When a negative thought enters your mind, immediately cancel it out with a positive thought.
4. Mentally minimize difficulties; maximize your strengths.
5. Deny the power of difficulty over you. Affirm the power of faith to overcome.
6. Believe in yourself.
7. Always be genuinely friendly.
8. Keep on learning, growing, improving yourself.
9. Build a ladder to your dreams—Determination
   Dedication
   Discipline
   Attitude
10. Every day practice the greatest of all positive affirmations, "I can do all things through Christ who strengthens me."

Norman Vincent Peale

THE VILLAGE BLACKSMITH

Under a spreading chestnut tree
  The village smithy stands;
The smith, a mighty man is he,
  With large and sinewy hands;
And the muscles of his brawny arms
  Are strong as iron bands.

His hair is crisp, and black and long
  His face is like the tan;
His brow is wet with honest sweat,
  He earns whate'er he can,
And looks the whole world in the face,
  For he owes not any man.

Week in, week out, from morn till night,
  You can hear his bellows blow;
You can hear him swing his heavy sledge,
  With measured beat and slow,
Like a sexton ringing the village bell,
  When the evening sun is low.

And children coming home from school
  Look in at the open door;
They love to see the flaming forge,
  And hear the bellows roar,
And catch the burning sparks that fly
  Like chaff from a threshing floor.

He goes on Sunday to the church,
  And sits among his boys;
He hears the parson pray and preach,
  He hears his daughter's voice,
Singing in the village choir,
  And it makes his heart rejoice.

It sounds to him like her mother's voice,
  Singing in Paradise!
He needs must think of her once more,
  How in the grave she lies;
And with his hard, rough hand he wipes
  A tear out of his eyes.

Toiling,—rejoicing,—sorrowing,
  Onward through life he goes;
Each morning sees some task begun,
  Each evening sees it close;
Somthing attempted, something done,
  Has earned a night's repose.

Thanks, thanks to thee, my worthy friend,
  For the lesson thou has taught!
Thus at the flaming forge of life
  Our fortunes must be wrought;
Thus on its sounding anvil shaped
  Each burning deed and thought.

Henry Wadsworth Longfellow

LEARN TO SEE

When he was born, George W. Campbell was blind. "Bilateral congenital cataracts," the doctor called it.

George's father looked at the doctor, not wanting to believe. "Isn't there anything you can do? Wouldn't an operation help?"

"No," said the doctor. "As of now, we know of no way to treat this condition."

George Campbell couldn't see, but the love and faith of his parents made his life rich. As a very young boy, he did not know that he was missing anything.

And then, when George was six years old, something happened which he wasn't able to understand. One afternoon he was playing with another youngster. The other boy, forgetting that George was blind, tossed a ball to him. "Look out! It'll hit you!"

The ball did hit George—and nothing in his life was quite the same after that. George was not hurt, but he was greatly puzzled. Later he asked his mother: "How could Bill know what's going to happen to me before I know it?"

His mother sighed, for now the moment she dreaded had arrived. Now it was necessary for her to tell her son for the first time: "You are blind." And here is how she did it:

"Sit down, George," she said softly as she reached over and took one of his hands. "I may not be able to describe it to you, and you may not be able to understand, but let me try to explain it this way." And sympathetically, she took one of his little hands in hers and started counting the fingers.

"One-two-three-four-five. These fingers are similar to what is known as the five senses." She touched each finger between her thumb and index finger in sequence as she continued the explanation.

"This little finger for hearing; this little finger for touch; this little finger for smell; this one for taste," and then she hesitated before continuing: "This little finger for sight. And each of the five senses, like each of the five fingers, sends messages to your brain."

Then she closed the little finger which she had named "sight" and tied it so that it would stay next to the palm of George's hand.

"George, you are different from other boys," she explained, "because you have the use of only four senses, like four fingers: one, hearing—two, touch—three, smell—and four, taste. But you don't have the use of your sense of sight. Now I want to show you something. Stand up," she said gently.

George stood up. His mother picked up his ball. "Now hold out your hand as if you were going to catch this," she said.

George held out his hands, and in a moment he felt the hard ball hit his fingers. He closed them tightly around it and caught it.

"Fine. Fine," said his mother. "I never want you to forget what you have just done. You can catch a ball with four fingers instead of five, George. You can also *catch* and *hold* a full and happy life with four senses instead of five—if you get in there and keep trying." Now George's mother had used a metaphor, and such a simple figure of speech is one of the quickest and most effective methods of communicating ideas between persons.

George never forgot the symbol of "four fingers instead of five." It meant to him the symbol of hope, and whenever he became discouraged because of his handicap, he used the symbol as a self-motivator. It became a form of self-suggestion to him. For he would repeat "four fingers instead of five" frequently. At times of need it would flash from his subconscious to his conscious mind.

And he found that his mother was right. He was able to catch a full life, and hold it with the use of the four senses which he did have.

But George Campbell's story doesn't end here.

In the middle of his junior year at high school the boy became ill, and it was necessary for him to go to the hospital. While George was convalescing, his father brought him information from which he learned that science had developed a cure for congenital cataracts. Of course, there was a chance of failure but—the chances for success far outweighed those for failure.

George wanted so much to see that he was willing to risk failure in order to see.

During the next six months four delicate surgical operations were performed—two on each eye. For days George lay in the darkened hospital room with bandages over his eyes.

And finally the day came for the bandages to be removed. Slowly, carefully, the doctor unwound the gauze from around George's head and over his eyes. There was only a blur of light.

George Campbell was still technically blind!

For one awful moment he lay thinking. And then he heard the doctor moving beside his bed. Something was being placed over his eyes.

"Now, can you see?" came the doctor's question.

George raised his head slightly from the pillow. The blur of light became color, the color a form, a figure.

"George!" a voice said. He recognized the voice. It was his mother's voice.

For the first time in his 18 years of life George Campbell was seeing his mother. There were the tired eyes, the wrinkled, 62-year-old face, and the knotted and gnarled hands. But to George she was most beautiful.

To him—she was an angel. The years of toil and patience, the years of teaching and planning, the years of being his seeing eyes, the love and affection: that was what George saw.

To this day he treasures his first visual picture: the sight of his mother. And, as you will see, he learned an appreciation for his sense of sight from this first experience.

"None of us can understand," he says, "the miracle of sight, unless we have had to do without it."

He will never forget the day he saw his mother standing before him in the hospital room, and did not know who she was—or even what she was—until he heard her speak. "What we see," George points out, "is always an interpretation of the mind. We have to train the mind to interpret what we see."

This observation is backed up by science. "Most of the process of seeing is not done by the eyes at all," says Dr. Samuel Renshaw, in describing the mental process of seeing. "The eyes act as hands which reach 'out there' and grab meaningless 'things' and bring them into the brain. The brain then turns the 'things' over to the memory. It is not until the brain interprets in terms of comparative action that we really *see* anything."

Some of us go through life "seeing" very little of the power and the glory around us. We do not properly filter the information that our eyes give us through the mental processes of the brain. As a result we often behold things without really *seeing* them at all. We receive physical impressions without grasping their meaning to us.

Is it time to have your mental vision checked? Not your physical vision—that is a matter for the medical specialists. But mental vision, like physical vision, can become distorted. When it does you can grope in a haze of false concepts . . . bumping and hurting yourself and others unnecessarily.

The most common physical weaknesses of the eye are two opposite extremes—nearsightedness and farsighted-ness. These are the major distortions of mental vision, too.

The person who is mentally nearsighted is apt to over-look objects and possibilities that are distant. He pays attention only to the problems immediately at hand and is blind to the opportunities that could be his by thinking and planning in terms of the future. You are nearsighted if you do not make plans, form objectives, and lay the foundation for the future.

On the other hand, the mentally farsighted person is apt to overlook possibilities that are right before him. He does not see the opportunities at hand. He sees only a dream-world of the future, unrelated to the present. He wants to start at the top rather than move up step by step—and he does not recognize that the only job where you can start at the top is the job of digging a hole.

Napoleon Hill and W. Clement Stone

Nothing in the world can take the place of persistence. Talent will not; nothing is more common than unsuccessful men with talent. Genius will not; genius is almost a proverb. Education will not; the world is full of education derelicts. Persistence and determination alone are omnipotent. The slogan, "Press On," has solved and always will solve the problem of the human race.

Calvin Coolidge

The greatest results in life are usually attained by simple means and the exercise of ordinary qualities. The common life of every day, with its cares, necessities and duties, affords ample opportunity for acquiring experience of the best kind; and its most beaten paths provide the true worker with abundant scope for effort and room for self-improvement. The road of human welfare lies along the old highway of steadfast well-doing; and they who are the most persistent, and work in the truest spirit, will usually be the most successful.

Fortune has often been blamed for her blindness, but fortune is not so blind as men are. Those who look into practical life will find that fortune is usually on the side of the industrious, as the winds and waves are on the side of the best navigators. In the pursuit of even the highest branches of human inquiry, the common qualities are found the most useful—such as common sense, attention, application and perseverance. Genius may not disdain the use of these ordinary qualities. The very greatest men have been among the least believers in the power of genius and have been as persevering as successful men of the common sort. Some have even defined genius to be only common sense intensified.

Newton's was unquestionably a mind of the very highest order, and yet when asked by what means he had worked out his extraordinary discoveries, he modestly answered, "By always thinking unto them." At another time he thus expressed his method of study: "I keep the subject continually before me and wait till the first dawnings open slowly by little and little into a full and clear light." It was in Newton's case as in every other only by diligent application and perseverance that his great reputation was achieved. Even his recreation consisted in change of study, laying down one subject and taking up another.

The extraordinary results effected by dint of sheer industry and perseverance have led many distinguished men to doubt whether the gift of genius be so exceptional an endowment as it is usually supposed to be. Thus Voltaire held that there is only a very slight line of separation that divides the man of genius from the man of ordinary mold. Locke, Helvetius and Diderot believed that all men have an equal aptitude for genius, and that what some are able to effect, under the laws which regulate the operations of the intellect, must also be within reach of others who, under like circumstances, apply themselves to like pursuits.

Dalton, the chemist, repudiated the notion of his being "a genius," attributing everything which he had accomplished to a simple industry and accumulation. We have, indeed, but to glance at the biographies of great men to find that the most distinguished inventors, artists, thinkers and workers of all kinds owe their success, in a great measure, to their indefatigable industry and application. They were men who turned all things to gold—even time itself. Disraeli the elder held that the secret of success consisted in being master of your subject, such mastery being attainable only through continuous application and study.

Hence, a great point to be aimed at is to get the working quality well trained. When that is done, the race will be found comparatively easy. We must repeat and again repeat: facility will come with labor. Not even the simplest art can be accomplished without it, and what difficulties it is found capable of achieving! It is indeed marvelous what continuous application will effect in the commonest of things.

Samuel Smiles

Ordinary abilities, coupled with application and perseverance, often achieve extraordinary results. *Fortune
favors the forearmed.* It is wonderful how the most serious
problems and difficulties are solved through earnest and
painstaking industry. The lives of the world's great men
are records of incessant and intelligent effort. *The power of
perseverance is incalculable.* It is an obvious truth that you
do not know what you can do until you try. It is equally
true that you cannot adequately estimate the great fields
open to you until you have ascended the heights for
advantageous observation. The capacity for hard work is
an element of genius. *There is really nothing too great for a
highly courageous mind.*

Grenville Kleiser

WORK

Place special emphasis upon the quality of your work. When the chief aim of your daily life is to produce intrinsically the best, and not merely the outwardly attractive, you can then afford to disregard the approval and praise of men. The inner consciousness of work worthily attempted and well done is its own reward. Let your thought be of quality, not quantity. To do good work you must be interested in it, and to be interested in it you must like it. All the master builders have been earnest, intense, conscientious workers. You can be one of the great men of the world, in the degree that you put quality into your daily work, seeking always for results rather than approbation. *Your opportunities are unlimited.*

Grenville Kleiser

Then a ploughman said, Speak to us of Work.

And he answered, saying:

You work that you may keep pace with the earth and the soul of the earth.

For to be idle is to become a stranger unto the seasons, and to step out of life's procession, that marches in majesty and proud submission towards the infinite.

When you work you are a flute through whose heart
the whispering of the hours turns to music.

Which of you would be a reed, dumb and silent, when
all else sings together in unison?

Always you have been told that work is a curse and a
labour a misfortune.

But I say to you that when you work you fulfill a part
of earth's furthest dream, assigned to you when that
dream was born,

And in keeping yourself with labour you are in truth
loving life,

And to love life through labour is to be intimate with
life's inmost secret.

But if you in your pain call birth an affliction and the
support of the flesh a curse written upon your brow, then
I answer that naught but the sweat of your brow shall
wash away that which is written.

You have been told also that life is darkness, and in
your weariness you echo what was said by the weary.

And I say that life is indeed darkness save when there
is urge,

And all urge is blind save when there is knowledge,

And all knowledge is vain save when there is work,

And all work is empty save when there is love;

And when you work with love you bind yourself to
yourself, and to one another, and to God.

And what is it to work with love?

It is to weave the cloth with threads drawn from your heart, even as if your beloved were to wear that cloth.

It is to build a house with affection, even as if your beloved were to dwell in that house.

It is to sow seeds with tenderness and reap the harvest with joy, even as if your beloved were to eat the fruit.

It is to charge all things you fashion with a breath of your own spirit,

And to know that all the blessed dead are standing about you and watching.

Often have I heard you say, as if speaking in sleep, "He who works in marble, and finds the shape of his own soul in the stone, is nobler than he who ploughs the soil.

And he who seizes the rainbow to lay it on a cloth in the likeness of man, is more than he who makes the sandals for our feet.

But I say, not in sleep but in the overwakefulness of noontide, that the wind speaks not more sweetly to the giant oaks than to the least of all the blades of grass;

And he alone is great who turns the voice of the wind into a song made sweeter by his own loving.

Work is love made visible.

And if you cannot work with love but only with distaste, it is better that you should leave your work and sit at the gate of the temple and take alms of those who work with joy.

For if you bake bread with indifference, you bake a bitter bread that feeds but half man's hunger.

And if you grudge the crushing of the grapes, your grudge distils a poison in the wine.

And if you sing though as angels, and love not the singing, you muffle man's ears to the voices of the day and the voices of the night.

Kahlil Gibran

If you work for a man, in heaven's name work for him. If he pays you wages that supply you your bread and butter, work for him, speak well of him, think well of him, stand by him, and stand by the institution he represents. I think if I worked for a man, I would work for him. I would not work for him a part of his time, but all of his time. I would give an undivided service or none. If put to a pinch, an ounce of loyalty is worth a pound of cleverness. If you must vilify, condemn and eternally disparage, why, resign your position and when you are outside, damn to your heart's content. But, I pray you, so long as you are part of an institution, do not condemn it. Not that you will injure the institution—not that—but when you disparage the concern of which you are a part, you disparage yourself. And don't forget, "I forgot" won't do in business.

Elbert Hubbard

The worst thing that can befall you is to have nothing useful to do. From that moment life will be an aimless, aching void, and time a cruel torturer. The man who has not experienced *the joy of hard work* has lived in vain. A life of ease and sloth is a daily purgatory and a cause of widespread unhappiness. It is incomprehensible that in this *day of golden opportunity* there should be anyone, in good health, with nothing to work and live for. The joy of work, of daily conquest, of unexpected difficulties overcome, of new enterprises—these make life interesting, worthwhile and wholesome. Find your right vocation, put your best abilities to daily use, work cheerfully, willingly, and courageously, and you will know *the joy of true living*.

Grenville Kleiser

GOSPEL OF LABOUR

This is the gospel of labour, ring it, ye bells of the kirk;
The Lord of Love came down from above, to live with
   the men who work.
This is the rose that he planted, here in the thorn-curst
   soil.
Heaven is blest with perfect rest, but the blessing of earth
   is toil.

Henry Van Dyke

Be your present work great or small the important thing is to do it well. Good work always confers a distinct benefit upon the worker. Greatness of spirit can make a little task great. Your visions of power and achievement are intimations of what you can be. They summon you to larger and more earnest effort. However well or much you have already done, you can do still better and more. *Immense possibilities are before you*, and the field of splendid opportunity widens as you persevere in honest purpose. Attempt the great, pursue the great, and ultimately you will achieve the great. Rise to your possibilities and know that through patient and persistent effort you can surely reach your *rightful place in the world*.

Grenville Kleiser

GOD'S OPEN DOOR
VIII

T HROUGH belief in God there are countless ways that we can open a door into bright spaces of spiritual bliss. Thanksgiving offers each of us the opportunity to show that we do indeed give thanks for our many blessings.

For more than thirty years, my family has sent Thanksgiving cards rather than Christmas cards to our friends, desiring to spread our gratitude for the many gifts of life. One year we included in our Thanksgiving mailing a parchment copy of the prayer of St. Francis suitable for framing, another year a complete copy of *The Greatest Thing on Earth* by Henry Drummond, and still another year the text of Ralph Waldo Trine's *In Tune with the Infinite*.

Like Thanksgiving, giving is an open door to greater spiritual enlightenment; so is forgiveness. We give of ourselves, we give thanks, and we learn to forgive ourselves and others.

The door is there for all of us to open.

THANKSGIVING

What is the shape of the future? As long as freedom
lives, the future is glorious.

When I was born in 1912 in Franklin County,
Tennessee, the United States had no color film . . . no
refrigerators . . . no radios . . . no transcontinental tele-
phones . . . no fluorescent lights . . . no traffic lights . . .
no talking pictures . . . no plastics . . . no human-made
fibers . . . no airplanes . . . no photocopiers . . . no fax
machines . . . no sports broadcasts . . . no antibiotics . . .
no herbicides . . . no nylon . . . no frozen foods . . . no
television . . . no transistors . . . no lasers . . . no genetic
engineering . . . no nuclear energy . . . and no human-
made satellites. The uniform wage for unskilled workers
was ten cents an hour. Now the average for factory
workers is ten dollars.

Even after adjusting for inflation, the increase is more
than tenfold. The federal budget in nominal dollars is
now almost three hundred times as great as at the peak of
prosperity in 1929. In my lifetime real consumption per
person worldwide—that is, the standard of living in real
goods—has more than quadrupled.

A landmark for freedom was the publication 214 years
ago of Adam Smith's great work called *An Inquiry into
the Nature and Causes of the Wealth of Nations.* In 214

years of relative freedom, the yearly output of goods and services worldwide has increased more than a hundred-fold. This is a hundredfold increase in real goods and services consumed, net after eliminating inflation.

Before Adam Smith, less than one thousand corporations existed on earth, but now corporations are being created at the rate of four thousand every business day. In the days of Adam Smith, 85 percent of the people were needed on the farm, but now less than 4 percent of the people on the farms in America produce a surplus of food.

We now enjoy prosperity greater than ever dreamed of before this century. Will this rate of progress continue in the future? If we are able to preserve and enhance freedom, these trends may continue and accelerate. We may expect more rapid change and wider fluctuations. Life will be full of adventure and opportunity and never be dull or routine.

In America alone this year over $100 billion will be dedicated to research and development—more in one year and in one nation than the total research for all the world's history before I was born. Awesome new blessings are visible also in health, entertainment, spiritual growth, and charity. In America alone over $100 billion will be donated to churches and charities this year. Each year the generous and voluntary giving by Americans alone exceeds the total income of all the world's people in any year before Adam Smith.

We should be overwhelmingly grateful to have been born in this century. The slow progess of prehistoric ages is over, and centuries of human enterprise are now miraculously bursting forth into flower. The evolution of human knowledge is accelerating, and we are reaping the fruits of generations of scientific thought: Only sixty years ago astronomers became convinced that the universe is 100 billion times larger than previously thought. More than half of the scientists who ever lived are alive today. More than half of the discoveries in the natural sciences have been made in this century. More than half of the goods produced since the earth was born have been produced in the two centuries since Adam Smith. Over half the books ever written were written in the last half-century. More new books are published each month than were written in the entire historical period before the birth of Columbus.

Discovery and invention have not stopped or even slowed down. Who can imagine what will be discovered if research continues to accelerate? Each discovery reveals new mysteries. The more we learn, the more we realize how ignorant we were in the past and how much more there is still to discover.

If you do not fall down on your knees each day, with overwhelming gratitude for your blessings—your multi-plying multitudes of blessings—then you just have not yet seen the big picture.

John Marks Templeton

I am thankful for small mercies. I compared notes with one of my friends who expects everything of the universe, and is disappointed when anything is less than the best; and I found that I begin at the other extreme, expecting nothing, and am always full of thanks for moderate goods. . . . In the morning I awake, and find the old world, wife, babes and mother, Concord and Boston, the dear old spiritual world, and even the dear old devil not far off. If we will take the good we find, asking no questions, we shall have heaping measures. The great gifts are not got by analysis. Everything good is on the highway.

Ralph Waldo Emerson

Our planet is a very good planet. In the first place, there is the alternation of night and day, and morning and sunset, and a cool evening following upon a hot day, and a silent and clear dawn presaging a busy morning, and there is nothing better than that. In the second place, there is the alternation of summer and winter, perfect in themselves, but made still more perfect by being gradually ushered in by spring and autumn, and there is nothing better than that. In the third place, there are the silent and dignified trees, giving us shade in summer and not shutting out the warm sunshine in winter, and there is nothing better than that. In the fourth place, there are flowers blooming and fruits ripening by rotations in the different months, and there is nothing better than that. In the fifth place, there are cloudy and misty days alternating with clear and sunny days, and there is nothing better than that. In the sixth place, there are spring showers and summer thunderstorms and the dry crisp wind of autumn

and the snow of winter, and there is nothing better than
that. In the seventh place, there are peacocks and parrots
and skylarks and canaries singing inimitable songs, and
there is nothing better than that. In the eighth place,
there is the zoo, with monkeys, tigers, bears, camels,
elephants, rhinoceros, crocodiles, sea lions, cows, horses,
dogs, cats, foxes, squirrels, woodchucks and more variety
and ingenuity than we ever thought of, and there is
nothing better than that. In the ninth place, there are
rainbow fish, swordfish, electric eels, whales, minnows,
clams, abalones, lobsters, shrimps, turtles and more
variety and ingenuity than we ever thought of, and there
is nothing better than that. In the tenth place, there are
magnificent redwood trees, fire-spouting volcanoes, magnificent caves, majestic peaks, undulating hills, placid
lakes, winding rivers and shady banks, and there is
nothing better than that. The menu is practically endless
to suit individual tastes, and the only sensible thing to do
is go and partake of the feast and not complain about the
monotony of life.

Lin Yutang

To be glad of life, because it gives you the chance to
love and to work and to play and to look up at the stars;
to be satisfied with your possessions, but not contented
with yourself until you have made the best of them; to
despise nothing in the world except falsehood and
meanness, and to fear nothing except cowardice; to be

governed by your admirations rather than by your disgusts; to covet nothing that is your neighbor's except his kindness of heart and gentleness of manner; to think seldom of your enemies, often of your friends and every day of Christ; and to spend as much time as you can with body and with spirit, in God's out-of-doors—these are little guideposts on the footpath of peace.

Henry Van Dyke

THE GETTYSBURG ADDRESS

Four-score and seven years ago our fathers brought forth on this continent a new nation conceived in liberty, and dedicated to the proposition that all men are created equal. Now we are engaged in a great civil war, testing whether that nation or any nation so conceived and so dedicated can long endure. We are met on a great battlefield of that war. We have come to dedicate a portion of that field as a final resting place for those who here gave up their lives that that nation might live. It is altogether fitting and proper that we should do this. But, in a larger sense, we cannot dedicate, we cannot conse- crate, we cannot hallow this ground. The brave men, living and dead, who struggled here, have consecrated it far above our poor power to add or detract. The world will little note nor long remember what we say here, but it can never forget what they did here. It is for us, the living, rather to be dedicated here to the unfinished work that they who fought here have thus far so nobly advanced. It is rather for us to be here dedicated to the great task remaining before us—that from these honored dead we take increased devotion to that cause for which they gave the last full measure of devotion; that we here highly resolve that these dead shall not have died in vain; that the nation, under God, shall have a new birth of freedom; and that the government of the people, by the people, for the people, shall not perish from the earth.

Abraham Lincoln

GIVING

Acquire the giving habit. Give intelligently, freely, liberally. Give money, books, merchandise, counsel, sympathy and inspiration. Give something every day. Cultivate the giving habit as you do the saving habit. *Give out of the fulness of your heart,* not with the expectation of return or gratitude, but because it is right to give. There is no greater joy in life than to render happiness to others by means of intelligent giving. Never before in the world has there been so much generous, sympathetic and unselfish service. It is the spirit of the supreme giver, the Christ who gave His life that men might know the way to the Father. You owe it to your highest self to *give every day as your are able.*

Grenville Kleiser

TEN POSITIVE COMMANDMENTS

I.   Thou shalt think well of thyself and well of thy neighbor.

II. Thou shalt add to the health, wealth and happiness of the world.

III. Thou shalt be on good terms with sunshine, fresh air and water.

IV. Thou shalt get eight hours' sleep a day.

V. Thou shalt eat moderately, and exercise every day in the open air.

VI. Thou shalt love the memory of thy mother, and be true to the friends that have done so much for thee.

VII. Thou shalt recognize the divinity in all men.

VIII. Thou shalt remember the week-day to keep it holy.

IX. Thou shalt remember that thee can only help thine by helping other people, and that to injure another is to injure thyself, and that to love and benefit others is to live long and well.

X. Thou shalt love the stars, the ocean, the forest, and reverence all living things, recognizing that the source of life is one.

Elbert Hubbard

To Give is to Receive is the law of Love. Under this law, when we give our Love away to others we gain, and what we give we simultaneously receive. The law of Love is based on abundance; we are completely filled with Love all the time, and our supply is always full and running

over. When we give our Love unconditionally to others
with no expectations of return, the Love within us
extends, expands and joins. So by giving our Love away
we increase the Love within us and everyone gains.

Gerald G. Jampolsky

There is no human possession so valuable as friendship.
It provides refuge, inspiration, solace, encouragement,
reasonable self-appreciation, as nothing else can do;
neither riches nor position, nor success, nor beauty, nor
health. Since friendship is so invaluable, it is worthwhile
to endeavor to understand its nature and to discover how
it can be secured. The quality of friendship varies with the
needs and the character of the individual. The friendship,
that we can each give, is something all our own and is in
many respects quite unlike the kind of friendship of
which another man is capable. There are friendships that
are entirely uncritical. To certain men their friends are
always above criticism. They are conscious only of their
fine qualities. They are literally blind to their faults. Such
a friendship is certainly pleasant to possess, and it often is
a reviving and stimulating influence, because most men
strive to be what their friends think they are. We may
know all about ourselves, we may thoroughly realize that
we are mean and cowardly and selfish, but, at the same
time, it is good for us to know that at least to one other
person we are something of a hero. We know that, if we

are found out, it will be bad for us, and will bring bitter
pain to the friend whose admiration we have learned to
value. Consequently there will always be a tendency to
strive against the meanness and the selfishness, and to
grow a little less unheroic, even though we may never be
numbered among the actual heroes. While, however,
undiscriminating friendship is not to be despised by the
person on whom it is bestowed, it is calculated in most
cases to become something of a tragedy for the friend
who gives it, because, sooner or later, faults become too
apparent to be ignored and love is saddened, if not
destroyed, by disillusion. Far more fortunate and, in the
long run, far more beneficient is the man who is capable
of critical friendship. With him affection and appreciation
can exist with clear knowledge of limitations and even
vices. Critical friendship depends on a god-like vision, on
a capacity, to see behind the superficial failings and to be
in touch with the fineness often hidden in the dross. . . .

Friendship is entirely mystical and not to be explained.
The wind bloweth where it listeth, and friendship cometh
where it will. In a sense, our friends force themselves
on us, obeying a law which neither they nor we can
understand or explain. . . .

It is dangerous to examine our friendships too closely.
It is disconcerting to be unable to find any reasonable
defence for a friendship that is a satisfaction and a joy.
Enjoyment of life to a large extent depends on friendship.
Without it, good times are dull and bad times are unendur-
able. It comes to us unsought, and it is given to us just
because we are ourselves, not for what we have, but for
what we are. . . .

To have a friend, one must be a friend. It is not only more blessed to give than to receive, but it is an undoubted fact that he who gives nothing will assuredly receive nothing. It is absolutely impossible to give to the non-giver. We live surrounded by people eager to be friendly though they may never become intimates. I have already referred to the amazing and wonderful kindness of the human race. The really unkind man who would rather be nasty than nice, who would rather hurt than help, who thoroughly enjoys making other people unhappy is rare and abnormal, and in a rationally regulated society, would be clapped into a lunatic asylum.

Sidney Dark

COUNT THAT DAY LOST

If you sit down at set of sun
And count the acts that you have done,
   And counting find
One self-denying deed, one word
That eased the heart of him who heard;
   One glance most kind
That fell like sunshine where it went—
Then you may count that day well spent.

But if, through all the livelong day,
You've cheered no heart, by yea or nay—
   If, through it all
You've nothing done that you can trace

That brought the sunshine to one face—
  No act most small
That helped some soul and nothing cost—
Then count that day as worse than lost.

George Eliot

GIVE

Give, and thou shalt receive. Give thoughts of cheer,
  Of courage and success, to friend and stranger.
And from a thousand sources, far and near,
  Strength will be sent thee in thy hour of danger.

Give words of comfort, of defense and hope,
  To mortals crushed by sorrow and by error.
And though thy feet through shadowy paths may grope,
  Thou shalt not walk in loneliness or terror.

Give of thy gold, though small thy portion be.
  Gold rusts and shrivels in the hand that keeps it.
It grows in one that opens wide and free.
  Who sows his harvest is the one who reaps it.

Give of thy love, nor wait to know the worth
  Of what thou lovest; and ask no returning.
And whereso'er thy pathway leads on earth,
  There thou shalt find the lamp of love-light burning.

Ella Wheeler Wilcox

He has achieved Success who has lived long, laughed often and loved much. Who has gained the trust of pure women, the respect of intelligent men, and the love of little children. Who has filled his niche and accomplished his task. Who has left the world better than he found it, whether by an improved poppy, a perfect poem or a rescued soul. Who has always appreciated earth's beauty and never failed to express it. Who has always looked for the best in others, and always given the best he had. Whose life was an inspiration; whose memory a benediction.

Author unknown

SYMPATHY, KNOWLEDGE AND POISE

Sympathy, Knowledge and Poise seem to be the three ingredients that are most needed in forming the Gentle Man. I place these elements according to their value. No man is great who does not have Sympathy plus, and the greatness of men can be safely gauged by their sympathies. Sympathy and imagination are twin sisters. Your heart must go out to all men, the high, the low, the rich, the poor, the learned, the unlearned, the good, the bad, the wise and the foolish—it is necessary to be one with them all, else you can never comprehend them. Sympathy!—it is the touchstone to every secret, the key to all knowledge, the open sesame of all hearts. Put yourself in the other man's place and then you will know why he thinks certain things and does certain deeds. Put yourself in his place and your blame will dissolve into pity, and your tears will wipe out the record of his misdeeds. The saviors of the world have simply been men with wondrous sympathy.

But knowledge must go with Sympathy, else the emotions will become maudlin and pity may be wasted on a poodle instead of a child; on a field-mouse instead of a human soul.

Knowledge in use is wisdom, and wisdom implies a sense of values—you know a big thing from a little one, a valuable fact from a trivial one. Tragedy and comedy are simply questions of value: a little misfit in life makes us laugh, a great one is tragedy and cause for expression of grief.

Poise is the strength of the body and strength of mind to control your Sympathy and your Knowledge. Unless you control your emotions they run over and you stand in the mire.

Sympathy must not run riot, or it is valueless and tokens weakness instead of strength. In every hospital for nervous disorders are to be found many instances of this loss of control. The individual has Sympathy but not Poise, and therefore his life is worthless to himself and to the world.

He symbols inefficiency and not helpfulness. Poise reveals itself more in voice than it does in words; more in thought than in action; more in atmosphere than in conscious life. It is a spiritual quality, and is felt more than it is seen. It is not a matter of bodily size, nor of bodily attitude, nor attire, nor of personal comeliness: it is a state of inward being, and of knowing your cause is just. And so you see it is a great and profound subject after all, great in its ramifications, limitless in extent, implying the entire science of right living. I once met a man who was deformed in body and little more than a dwarf, but who had such Spiritual Gravity—such Poise— that to enter a room where he was, was to feel his presence and acknowledge his superiority. To allow Sympathy to waste itself on unworthy objects is to deplete one's life forces. To conserve is the part of wisdom, and reserve is a necessary element in all good literature, as well as in everything else.

Poise being the control of our Sympathy and Knowl-edge, it implies a possession of these attributes, for without having Sympathy and Knowledge, you have nothing to control but your physical body. To practise Poise as a mere gymnastic exercise, or study in etiquette, is to be self-conscious, stiff, preposterous and ridiculous. Those who cut such fantastic tricks before high heaven as make angels weep, are men void of Sympathy and Knowledge trying to cultivate Poise. Their science is a mere matter of what to do with arms and legs. Poise is a question of spirit controlling flesh, heart controlling attitude.

Get Knowledge by coming close to Nature. That man is the greatest who best serves his kind. Sympathy and Knowledge are for use—you acquire that you may give out; you accumulate that you may bestow. And as God has given unto you the sublime blessings of Sympathy and Knowledge, there will come to you the wish to reveal your gratitude by giving them out again; for the wise man is aware that we retain spiritual qualities only as we give them away. Let your light shine. To him that hath shall be given. The exercise of wisdom brings wisdom; and at the last the infinitesimal quantity of man's Knowledge compared with the Infinite, and the smallness of man's Sympathy when compared with the source from which ours is absorbed, will evolve an abnegation and a humility that will lend a perfect Poise. The Gentleman is a man with perfect Sympathy, Knowledge, and Poise.

Elbert Hubbard

One of the laws of the spirit seems to be that self-improvement comes mainly from trying to help others—especially from trying to help others to enjoy spiritual growth. Growth comes by humbly seeking to be a more useful tool in God's hands. Giving material things to others helps the growth of the givers but often injures the receivers. It is better to help the receivers to find ways to grow spiritually themselves. It is more farsighted to give advice and instruction, like a wise father to the son whom he loves. If, following Jesus, we teach "Seek ye first the Kingdom of God," then the other material things will follow. Helping the poor to grow spiritually and to become givers themselves is the only real road to permanent riches, including material riches.

John Marks Templeton

WHICH ARE YOU?

There are two kinds of people on earth to-day;
Just two kinds of people, no more, I say.

Not the sinner and the saint, for it's well understood,
The good are half bad, and the bad are half good.

Not the rich and the poor, for to rate a man's wealth,
You must first know the state of his conscience and
    health.

Not the humble and proud, for in life's little span,
Who puts on vain airs, is not counted a man.

Not the happy and sad, for the swift flying years
Bring each man his laughter and each man his tears.

No; the two kinds of people on earth I mean,
Are the people who lift and the people who lean.

Wherever you go, you will find the earth's masses
Are always divided in just these two classes.

And, oddly enough, you will find too, I ween,
There's only one lifter to twenty who lean.

In which class are you? Are you easing the load
Of overtaxed lifters, who toil down the road?

Or are you a leaner, who lets others share
Your portion of labor, and worry and care?

Ella Wheeler Wilcox

They said of him, about the city that night, that it was
the peacefullest man's face ever beheld there. Many added
that he looked sublime and prophetic.

One of the most remarkable sufferers by the same axe—
a woman—had asked at the foot of the same scaffold, not
long before, to be allowed to write down the thoughts
that were inspiring her. If he had given any utterance to
his, and they were prophetic, they would have been these:

"I see a beautiful city and a brilliant people rising from
this abyss, and, in their struggles to be truly free, in their
triumphs and defeats, through long years to come, I see
the evil of this time and of the previous time of which
this is the natural birth, gradually making expiation for
itself and wearing out.

"I see the lives for which I lay down my life, peaceful,
useful, prosperous and happy, in that England which I
shall see no more. I see her with a child upon her bosom,
who bears my name. I see her father, aged and bent, but
otherwise restored, and faithful to all men in his healing
office, and at peace. . . .

"I see that I hold a sanctuary in their hearts, and in the
hearts of their descendants, generations hence. . . .

"I see that child who lay upon her bosom and who
bore my name, a man winning his way up in that path of
life which once was mine. I see him winning it so well,
that my name is made illustrious there by the light of his.
I see the blots I threw upon it, faded away. I see him,
foremost of just judges and honoured men, bringing a
boy of my name, with a forehead that I know and golden

hair, to this place, then fair to look upon, with not a trace of this day's disfigurement—and I hear him tell the child my story, with a tender and faltering voice.

"It is a far, far better thing that I do, than I have ever done; it is a far, far better rest that I go to, than I have ever known."

Charles Dickens, in
A Tale of Two Cities

FORGIVENESS

With peace of mind as our single goal, forgiveness becomes our single function. Forgiveness is the vehicle used for correcting our misperceptions and for helping us let go of fear. Simply stated, to forgive is to let go.

Our first step in mind retraining is to establish peace of mind as our single goal. This means thinking of ourselves first in terms of self-fullness, not selfishness. The second step is forgiveness.

Many of us become frustrated when we make the mistake of trying to love others as the first step. In light of our past distorted values and experiences, some people simply seem unlovable; because of our faulty perception of their behavior it is difficult to love them.

When we have peace of mind as a single goal, we can then take the second step, forgiveness, and choose to see others as extending Love, or being fearful and calling for help in the form of Love. With this new perception, it becomes easier to give both total Love and acceptance to the other person and therefore to experience inner peace at the same time.

Gerald G. Jampolsky

Because of Jesus, I believe in forgiveness—in the forgiveness of God to man, and from man to man, and from me to anyone who needs forgiveness.

I believe that love is stronger than all other forces— that to love is better than to be angry; that it is better to give than to receive; better to serve than to be served; better to forget myself than to assert myself.

I believe that God's kingdom can come on earth, and that everything that is wrong in the life of the nation, or of the church, or in my life can be conquered by the power of God.

I believe that nothing that is wrong need be permanent.

A. Herbert Gray

THE TRUE GENTLEMAN

It is almost a definition of a gentleman to say that he is one who never inflicts pain. This description is both refined and, as far as it goes, accurate. He is mainly occupied in merely removing the obstacles which hinder the free and unembarrassed action of those about him; and he concurs with their movements rather than takes the initiative himself. His benefits may be considered as parallel to what are called comforts or conveniences in arrangements of a personal nature: like an easy chair or a good fire, which do their part in dispelling cold and fatigue, though nature provides both means of rest and animal heat without them. The true gentleman in like manner carefully avoids whatever may cause a jar or a jolt

in the minds of those with whom he is cast;—all clashing
of opinion, or collision of feeling, all restraint, or suspicion, or gloom, or resentment; his great concern being
to make everyone at their ease and at home. He has his
eyes on all his company; he is tender towards the bashful,
gentle towards the distant, and merciful towards the
absurd; he can recollect to whom he is speaking; he
guards against unreasonable allusions, or topics which
may irritate; he is seldom prominent in conversation, and
never wearisome. He makes light of favours while he does
them, and seems to be receiving when he is conferring.
He never speaks of himself except when compelled, never
defends himself by a mere retort, he has no ears for
slander or gossip, is scrupulous in imputing motives to
those who interfere with him, and interprets everything
for the best. He is never mean or little in his disputes,
never takes unfair advantage, never mistakes personalities
or sharp sayings for arguments, or insinuates evil which
he dare not say out. From a long-sighted prudence, he
observes the maxim of the ancient sage, that we should
even conduct ourselves towards our enemy as if he were
one day to be our friend. He has too much good sense
to be affronted at insults, he is too well employed to
remember injuries, and too indolent to bear malice. He
is patient, forbearing and resigned, on philosophical principles; he submits to pain, because it is inevitable, to
bereavement, because it is irreparable, and to death,
because it is his destiny. If he engages in controversy of
any kind his disciplined intellect preserves him from the
blundering discourtesy of better, perhaps, but less edu-
cated minds; who, like blunt weapons, tear and hack

instead of cutting clean, who mistake the point in argument, waste their strength on trifles, misconceive their adversary and leave the question more involved than they find it. He may be right or wrong in his opinion, but he is too clearheaded to be unjust; he is as simple as he is forcible, and as brief as he is decisive. Nowhere shall we find greater candour, consideration, indulgence: he throws himself into the minds of his opponents, he accounts for their mistakes. He knows the weakness of human reason as well as its strength.

John Henry Cardinal Newman

Author Index

279

INDEX BY TITLES
OR FIRST LINES

281

Topical Index

ACKNOWLEDGMENTS

Grateful acknowledgment is made to the following authors, agents, publishers, and other copyright holders for the use of the material quoted in this book. Every effort has been made to locate copyright holders and, if any material has been used without proper permission, the editor would appreciate being notified so that proper credit can be given in future editions.

From *Cosmic Consciousness* by Richard Maurice Bucke. Copyright © 1901, 1923 by E. P. Dutton & Co. Reprinted by permission of the publisher E. P. Dutton, a division of NAL Penguin Inc.

From *Love* by Leo F. Buscaglia. Copyright © 1972 by Leo F. Buscaglia, Inc. Excerpted by permission.

From *Life Is For Loving* by Eric Butterworth. Copyright © 1973 by Eric Butterworth. Reprinted by permission of Harper & Row, Publishers, Inc.

From *Unity* magazine, by Sue Crawford, January 1987, reprinted by permission of author.

From *What Do You Really Want For Your Children?* by Dr. Wayne Dyer. Copyright © 1985 by Dr. Wayne W. Dyer. Reprinted by permission of William Morrow & Co., Inc.

From *Choosing Your Own Greatness* by Dr. Wayne W. Dyer. Reprinted by permission of Nightingale-Conant, an audio cassette program © Nightingale-Conant Corp, 1987.

"I Am God's Melody of Life" by Georgiana Tree West. Reprinted by permission.

From *Unity* magazine, "Christmas—Its Scientific Meaning" by Charles Fillmore. Reprinted by permission of *Unity*.

From *Sparks of Truth* by Emmet Fox. Copyright © 1941 by Emmet Fox. Reprinted by permission of Harper & Row Publishers, Inc. British and Commonwealth rights by permission of Blanche Wolhorn.

From various books, magazines, and lecture sources by permission of James Dillet Freeman.

From *The Prophet* by Kahlil Gibran. Reprinted by permission of Alfred A. Knopf, Inc. Copyright © 1923 by Kahlil Gibran and renewed © 1951 by Administrators C.T.A. of the Estate of Kahlil Gibran and Mary G. Gibran.

From *It's My Turn* by Ruth Bell Graham. Copyright © 1982 by Ruth Bell Graham. Used by permission of Fleming H. Revell Company. Rights excludinig USA, Philippines, and Canada by permission of Hodder & Stoughton, Ltd.

From *Success Through a Positive Mental Attitude* by Napoleon Hill and W. Clement Stone. Copyright © 1960 by Napoleon Hill and W. Clement Stone. Used by permission of the publisher, Prentice-Hall, Inc., Englewood Cliffs, NJ

From *Love is Letting Go of Fear* by Gerald G. Jampolsky. Copyright © 1979 by Gerald G. Jampolsky, M.D. Published by Celestial Arts. Reprinted by permission of author.

From *The Book of Hymns* by Abingdon Press Harmonization copyright ©1964 by Abingdon Press (#34 *The Book of Hymns*). Used by permission.

From *30-Day Mental Diet* by Willis Kinnear. Copyright © 1963 by Willis Kinnear. Reprinted by permission of Science of Mind Pub.

From *Mere Christianity* by C. S. Lewis. Copyright © 1952 by William Collins Sons & Co., Ltd. Reprinted by permission of William Collins Sons & Co., Ltd. and the Estate of C. S. Lewis.

From *The Spirit of St. Louis* by Charles A. Lindbergh. Copyright © 1953 Charles Scribner's Sons; copyright renewed © 1981 Anne Morrow Lindbergh. Reprinted with the permission of Charles Scribner's Sons, an imprint of Macmillan Publishing Company. Rights (excluding USA, its territories, and dependencies, and Canada) throughout the world by permission of John Murray (Publishers) Ltd.

From *Conjectures of a Guilty Bystander* by Thomas Merton. Copyright © 1965, 1966 by The Abbey of Gethsemani. Reprinted by permission of Doubleday, a division of Bantam, Doubleday, Dell Publishing Group, Inc.

From *A Gift For God* by Mother Teresa. Copyright © 1975 by Mother Teresa Missionaries of Charity. Reprinted by permission of Harper & Row, Publishers, Inc.

Acknolwedgements

From *The Art of Contrary Thinking* by Humphrey B. Neill. Copyright © 1954 by Humphrey B. Neill. Reprinted by permission of the Caxton Printers, Ltd.

From *The Positive Power of Jesus Christ* by Norman Vincent Peale.

From *Why Some Positive Thinkers Get Positive Results* by Norman Vincent Peale. Copyright © 1986 by Norman Vincent Peale. Reprinted by permission of Thomas Nelson Publishers.

From *The Peter Prescription* by Laurence J. Peter. Copyright © 1972 by Laurence J. Peter. Reprinted by permission of William Morrow and Co., Inc.

From *Unity* magazine by G. Richard Rieger, reprinted by permission of author and Unity School of Christianity.

From *Overcoming Indecisiveness* by Theodore Isaac Rubin. Copyright © 1985 by Theodore Isaac Rubin. Reprinted by permission of Harper & Row, Publishers, Inc.

From *You Can Become the Person You Want To Be* by Robert H. Schuller. Copyright © 1973 by Robert H. Schuller. A Hawthorn Book, reprinted by permission of E. P. Dutton, a division of NAL Penguin Inc. British rights by permission of Robert H. Schuller.

From *On Happiness* by Pierre Teilhard de Chardin. U.S. rights by permission of Harper & Row, Inc. Canadian and British Commonwealth rights by permission of Editions du Seuil.

From *The Shaking of the Foundations* by Paul Tillich. Copyright © 1948 Charles Schribner's Sons; copyright renewed © 1976 Hannah Tillich. Reprinted by permission of Charles Schribner's Sons, an imprint of Macmillan Publishing Company. British Commonwealth rights, excluding Canada, by permission of S.C.M. Press

From *In Tune With the Infinite* by Ralph Waldo Trine. Reprinted by permission of Macmillan Publishing Company. Copyright © 1921, 1928, 1929, 1936 by Ralph Waldo Trine. Copyright © 1957, 1970 by Macmillan Publishing Company.

From *The Importance of Living* by Lin Yutang. Reprinted by permission of Taivi Lin Lai and Hsiang Ju Lin.

From *The Joy of Working* by Denis Waitley and Reni L. Witt. Copyright © 1985 by Larimi Communications Associates, Inc. Reprinted by permission of Dodd, Mead & Company, Inc.